THE CONNOISSEUR NEW GUIDES

Antique English Furniture

Uniform with this volume:

ANTIQUE ENGLISH POTTERY, PORCELAIN AND GLASS

A vermilion lacquer cabinet on an elaborately carved gilt wood stand, *c.* 1675.
Ht 5 ft 9 in. *Mallett and Son, London.*

THE CONNOISSEUR NEW GUIDE TO

Antique English

FURNITURE

Edited by L. G. G. Ramsey, Editor of *The Connoisseur*

With an Introduction by Terence Davis

E. P. DUTTON & COMPANY INC., NEW YORK

Designed and produced for E. P. DUTTON & CO. INC.
by Rainbird, McLean Ltd, 11 Charlotte Street, London W1
First Published in the U.S.A., 1961 by E. P. Dutton & Co. Inc.

Printed in England

Contents

Introduction

This is the first in a series of monographs on English antiques. It is a book for the collector who requires a compact and well-illustrated guide to the various styles encountered in the study of English furniture.

Most of the furniture illustrated and mentioned in the text is of a quality beyond the means of the average collector, and much of it, indeed, now takes pride of place in museums and important private collections. But this is a *guide to style*, without a knowledge of which no collector can enter an antique shop or bid at a sale, even though the piece he wants may not be the same quality as many of the pieces illustrated here. The furniture collector, in his ascent to the status of connoisseur, may, however, safely start on his career of educative mistakes and small triumphs with a seeing eye for good proportion and seemly design, in whatever period he chooses to collect.

On first examination it appears that the history of English furniture can be neatly arranged into precise compartments of time: Tudor, Stuart, Early Georgian, Late Georgian, Regency, Early Victorian (the order in which we present the various periods in this book). Then we find that, to some degree, each period is one of transition. Sometimes, particularly in the country houses of the nobility, we find a room completely furnished in one period. Yet most houses contained, and still do, examples of furniture or different styles and dates. The complete Kent, Adam or Duncan Phyfe room exists, but it is very much the exception.

There are, however, certain dates and events that help to explain the changes and developments that occurred and show that furniture was elaborated and assumed certain forms for a number of different reasons. The materials used were an important influence on the evolution of furniture design. Mahogany, for example, began to be used in quantity from about 1725 and soon superseded walnut in general use – partly because stocks of seasoned walnut were decreasing, but also because it had been in use since the Restoration and the moment for a change had arrived. Cabinet-makers also found that mahogany had distinct advantages over walnut. It could be cut in larger sections. It could be carved more crisply; and it was much stronger, especially for chair legs. It offered more opportunities for refinement of detail and the development of more sophisticated styles.

Knowledge confined to that which is directly relevant to a particular period or piece of furniture, tends to become mere specialization, but it is almost impossible for the lively-minded collector not to go beyond these narrow confines. The whole way of life of any generation can be read from the shape and character of the domestic things which they used and the buildings that they fashioned to contain them. John Gloag in his *English Furniture* writes: "When people have understood the art of living, they have left behind the graceful things—furniture of intrinsic dignity and a quiet pattern of beauty in the surroundings they created. In our [present] age, concern with efficiency in living, in the mechanistic and hygienic sense, may for ever preclude us from the full enjoyment of leisure . . . our furniture betrays our ideas to posterity in even greater detail than our architecture." So it was with earlier periods; from the time when furnishings were confined to the essentials of a rough working life to the fashion-bound trappings of Stuart, Georgian and Regency days.

The background against which any distinctive style of furniture may be set can be summarized briefly as follows: the circumstances of daily life (whether governed by peace or war); the architecture of the period; the influence of individual architects, artists and craftsmen; the state of communications and transport; the kind of communities in which people lived; and major and often comparatively minor historical events.

The pursuit of the antiques requires not merely knowledge but also constant application, time, money, and a certain instinct. High prices, and the rarity of genuine early pieces have directed some collectors to consider the possibilities of later work, and, although this does not directly concern us here, the best of twentieth-century furniture is quite eagerly sought today as the antique of the future. But whatever period or kind of furniture is chosen by a collector on however modest a scale, knowledge is acquired by experience and *looking*. Many countries are fortunate in their museums, country houses or castles open to the public. Auction rooms and dealers' galleries are other places where the enthusiastic amateur may look and learn.

Provided one has certain basic knowledge, it is comparatively easy to detect fakes or pieces which have been "altered". Invariably it is the *surface* of a piece that indicates age, and it is this that the study or collector should first examine. It is almost impossible for a faker to give the appearance of genuine age and patinated surface. The patina of age and years of polishing cannot be artificially created. Some antique furniture today is sold as "restored". In such cases the good dealer will be ready to point out the extent of the restoration. This should have been done with care and skill. There are also finely-made nineteenth-century copies of eighteenth-century pieces. These are sold by the good dealer for what they are.

Deviations in style, workmanship and materials in any period may be explained in part by remembering that social conditions dictated that furniture-making should necessarily pursue different courses: luxurious work for the palaces and great country houses, and cruder work by local craftsmen for the more humble homes of country dwellers. There was little between "furniture" until the merchant classes became established. Again, because transport was slow and infrequent, ideas percolated slowly from London to provincial centres and local craftsmen would continue furniture styles long out of fashion in London. In the country, also, the traditional, easily available woods would continue in use: oak, during the greater part of the seventeenth century, as well as yew, ash, elm and fruit woods. For the collector this means that original work said to be by well-known London cabinet-makers is now much sought after and consequently expensive. Yet more reasonably priced pieces, made *in the same style* some years later by country craftsmen, can be found. They are worth looking for, and possess a robust if naïve character which furniture of superior quality lacks.

This volume is divided into the six important periods of English furniture, and provides the connoisseur and amateur enthusiast alike with a convenient guide to chronology and evolution.

Terence Davis

TUDOR

In every household from manor-house and merchant's residence to princely palace in sixteenth-century England the pattern of domestic economy was more or less the same. The rooms followed the same order from hall door to attics, their relationship to one another was the same, and they were used for the same purposes. They were larger or smaller according to circumstances, and in the great houses the chambers in the private apartments were more numerous. The daily life of the inhabitants was not, of course, in every case ordered on precisely the same lines, but was arranged with increasing ceremony as the rank and wealth of the owner rose. It is therefore no matter for surprise that when we examine the inventories of the furniture of the houses of the middle and upper classes of this period we find the same pattern recurring again and again. Given any room and its dimensions, it is possible to say almost exactly how and with what pieces of furniture it would have been garnished. Joseph Nash's *Mansions of England* made an earlier generation familiar with the appearance of the interiors of Knole, of Hardwick and of Haddon Hall as they existed in the second quarter of the nineteenth century. But Nash furnished them very much to suit the romantic taste of his age. More people than ever before are now familiar with their present appearance. And by combining fact with fiction the film-screen has accustomed us to what producers fondly believe are typical Tudor interiors. Such reconstructions of the interiors of the greater houses may sufficiently serve their purpose but it is very doubtful if a "Tudor" or "Elizabethan" room, in the sense meant by the period furnishers of today, ever had any real existence in the homes of the sixteenth century. Apart from the built-in aumbries and the wallseats, and the panelling – which were part of the house when it was first set up – the movables were an agglomeration brought together over a period of perhaps a hundred years. New pieces were added or old ones were replaced, as the need arose. The day when a Benedict brought his bride home to a house in which the principal rooms were filled with new furniture had not yet dawned.

The furniture in the principal rooms of an early Tudor house must have been a pleasing mixture of the late Gothic and the early Renaissance; but by the time that the then owner's grandson had come into possession, the gothic relics had no doubt been banished to the lesser rooms and the domestic offices, and what was left, with the addition of new pieces, must still have been a mellow hotch-potch of styles– set against the old panelling and its immovables.

Dr Andrew Boorde in his *Dyetorie or Regiment of Healthe*, 1547, recapitulates the principles to be observed when laying out a house. There is, however, nothing new in his plan, since it is the same one on which all houses from the franklin's farm to the baronial residence in the fourteenth century were arranged. "Make the hall", he says, "of such fashion that the parlour be annexed to the head of the hall, and the buttrye and pantrye at the lower ende thereof; the cellar under the pan- trye sett somewhat at a base; the kechyn sett somewhat at a base from the buttrye and pantrye; coming with an entrie within by the wall of the buttrie; the pastrie house and the larder annexed to the kechyn." But Boorde clearly envisages a much more ambitious building. After some words on the position of the gate-house, he goes on: "Let the prevye chamber be annexed to the great chamber of estate, with other chambers necessary for the buildinge". He is here thinking of such palatial residences as Hampton Court, wherein the functions of the hall and the parlour were split up among other chambers such as the presence chamber or great chamber of estate, the dining-room and the withdrawing room; the hall being used only for special festivities such as those of Christmas and Easter.

To illustrate the manner in which such a house was furnished there is the inven- tory of the contents of a moderately sized house, that of Sir William More of Loseley, the contents of which were scheduled in 1556. It was a typical house of the period in which the domestic economy system of the century had reached its complete development. The organization and arrangement of the house are clear- cut and sharply defined. They are not blurred by the ceremonial of a Hatfield nor reduced to the minimum as, for example, in the case of a working weaver's house at Biddenden in Kent, of which we also possess particulars.

The Interior of Loseley House. When the hall door shut behind the visitor he found himself in a long, narrow passage that crossed the house from side to side and led to the kitchen and domestic offices, one wall being one of the main walls of the house, while the other was a wainscotted screen, the "spere" of the Middle Ages, pierced with two doorways, usually one at either end, which opened into the hall. There was no furniture in this narrow passage-way, and it was unlit except by perhaps a pair of sconces or flambeaux.

On passing through one of the doorways in the screen the visitor entered the hall. Its arrangement and furnishing followed a common plan. Its most prominent feature was the large chair of the master of the house standing upon the dais or raised platform at the top of the room. Before this stood the high table, the table dormant of Chaucer's franklin, while behind it, if the owner's rank warranted it, hung a cloth of estate embroidered with his coat-armour. To one side of the chair was perhaps a second and lesser one for the lady of the house, though in general she would be accommodated with a stool. And when the family dined, they and such guests as might be present at the high table were provided with stools. To one side of the dais stood a cup-board on which the appointments for the high table were kept. At the lower end of the hall, between the two doorways in the screen, stood a hutch table, the ancestor of the modern sideboard, acting as a serving-table on which the dishes or messes were placed as they were brought in from the kitchen, and from which they were distributed to those at the high and the other tables by servants. Against the wall opposite the windows were high-backed benches, which were garnished as necessary with bankers and cushions for comfort. Between them was the fireplace and perhaps facing it a settle.

As the entire household dined together, temporary tables, boards with supporting trestles, were placed in position down the hall, and the necessary forms and stools grouped about them. But by the early sixteenth century these removable tables were already tending to give place to fixed standing tables, with forms at the sides, while the stools were nested underneath them until required. At the side of the room stood one or more livery cupboards or hutches.

The only shortcoming in this pleasant scene of well-ordered domesticity was the floor of the hall. Erasmus, who lived for some years in England in the early part of the sixteenth century, and knew both great houses like that of Sir Thomas More in Chelsea and the Colleges at Cambridge, as well as those of lesser standing, had a very poor opinion of the way in which English halls were floored and the way in which they were generally kept. It is difficult to believe that the hall of the author of *Utopia* was of the kind he describes, but his findings were undoubtedly true of many another. They were, he says, laid with white clay and covered with rushes, of which the upper layers were renewed with reasonable regularity. The lower, however, remained undisturbed sometimes for as much as twenty years, and harboured in their depths the abominations that should by rights have been swallowed by the cess-pit. Much that in the then prevailing way of life should have been emptied into the kennels was spilt upon the hall floor, covered with fresh rushes, and the stench concealed as far as possible by a generous sprinkling of sweet-smelling herbs. But this was not so in the private chambers, where tiled floors were common on the ground level and boarded ones above. Such were the bare furnishings of the hall. But this somewhat austere picture must be completed by the addition of wall-paintings above the panelling, tapestries or painted cloths and stained glass in the windows. Portraits and other decorative paintings added to the attractiveness of an interior. "Tables of the Royal Arms" are frequently mentioned in inventories, and were displayed not to bolster up a claim to kinship with the Sovereign but as a gesture of loyalty. Inventories make frequent mention of a few weapons in the hall, and these were undoubtedly kept there as a precaution against a forced entry; for every man in those days was his own constable and was prepared to meet violence with arms in his hands. But certainly relics of half-forgotten battles, or the ancient harness of an ancestor, might well be hung up for monuments, and they are described as being so displayed in the song *The Old and the New Courtier.*

The parlour. At the upper end of the hall and to the side of the dais a doorway opened on a short passage to the private rooms of the family. Out of one side of this passage was the staircase to the upper floor, and just beyond was the parlour the sitting-room of the family. So far as can be judged from the rather bare record in the inventory, More's parlour was well furnished. Firstly there was "a table of Chesnut wt a frame joyned to the same", evidently a fairly large table that could be used as a dining-table when Sir William wished to entertain his guests in private. There was "one joyned cheyre' for Sir William and "vj joyned stoles of chesnut" for the rest of his family or guests, with a supply of "footstoles". There was "a lyttle joyned table" for occasional purposes, and "a syde-table joyned", which was possibly a so-called "credence table." There was also a chess-board.

Beyond the parlour were two small rooms, the closets respectively of Sir William and Lady More. The first was devoted principally to the business of the estate, and in many old houses such a room is still called the Justice Room, because in it were disentangled the many problems that arose between the master and his tenants and his household servants. It was the room in which tenants paid their rents, and those in charge of the affairs of the house and the home farm rendered their accounts. Its impedimenta, of which a very full list is given in the inventory, reflect these activities. Firstly there was a "counter bord of chesnut tree", which was undoubtedly a counting table, perhaps incised on the top with a chequer design on which the counters or jettons were shuffled in casting accounts. Unmarked examples when in use were covered with a green baize cloth embroidered with the necessary chequers. For smaller sums there was "a slate to wryte in" with "a pinne of bone to wryte wt", and "a pene of yron" and two desks. No chair or stools are listed. It would seem these were brought in from the parlour when required. There are no presses or hutches to house Sir William's fairly extensive library of some hundred and thirty books. Some of these from their titles were evidently acquired for their usefulness in solving daily problems. Others hint at More's interest in history and geography, and the remainder are classics, or works of entertainment. Lady More's closet on the other hand was devoted to the domestic economics of the household, and was at the same time equipped to attend to minor ailments or accidents. Beside the bare necessities of a table and stool the only furnishings were shelves upon which stood flagons and jars of unguents and simples.

Beyond these rooms, if the size of the house and the position of the master warranted it, was the chapel, which generally occupied the end of one or the other wing of the house. It was generally two floors high, and on the upper floor the room behind it often lacked the wall between it and the chapel, so that a rail across the open side converted it into a watching chamber for the family.

Back from the chapel on the upper floor a gallery led to the stairs, and off this were the great bedrooms, that of the master, and beyond it that of the mistress. The movables in Sir William More's bedroom – "The chamber wherein I lye" – were not as numerous as one might have expected. The inventory merely lists a "joyned bed", "a square table of walnut tree", a "lyttle joyned chayre", "another joyned chayre", and "iij joyned stoles of chesnuttree for women". The table and one of the chairs stood normally at the head of the bed, one at each side, the one supporting the nightlight or watch, a cup and a flagon of wine in case of need. In the morning they were no doubt moved to the centre of the room or over to the fireplace, where they joined company with the other chair and the stools, when the master in his night- or chamber-gown broke his fast in the company of his wife and her ladies.

Such a chamber usually also contained a chest for valuables placed at the foot of the bed, where it served as a seat, and a second one for clothes and linen.

> In cypress chests my arras counterpoints,
> Costly apparel, tents and canopies,
> Fine linen, Turkey cushions boss'd with pearl,
> Valance of Venice gold in needle work,
> Pewter and brass, and all things that belong
> To house or housekeeping.
> *Taming of the Shrew*, 1594–1600, Act II.

The utensils for washing were either a two-spouted hanging laver with its basin in an iron stand, or an ewer and basin which, when not in use, stood upon a cupboard.

Of immovables there were probably one or two wall-benches and perhaps a press for clothes set in the wall.

If not an aumbry, there was probably an alcove hidden behind a curtain with a bench or transverse rod from which garments could be hung, the ancestor of the modern built-in clothes cupboard.

The children's chamber at Loseley was apparently furnished purely as a night nursery. There was no table, or chair: not even a stool. The inventory lists only a "bedsted joyned", for the nurse and her older charges, and "a credell" for the youngest. "A joyned cup-board" was doubtless used for the storage of any necessaries in the way of platters, an ewer, basin and so forth. Clothing and extra bed-linen was kept in the "cofere with a lock" and the second "cofere without a lock", which acted as seats when necessary. The furnishings were completed by "ij lettle close-stoles", evidently to meet the requirements of the children.

Back on the ground floor and in the Hall, through the screen and at the end of the entrance passage, were the pantry and buttery and the wine-cellar, and beyond them the kitchen with the stillroom and dairy. Some of the male servants slept in the pantry and buttery on pallet beds, a practice that continued until the nineteenth century. Above were the attics where the servant-maids slept. Outside were the stables, with rooms above for the grooms, the coachman if there was one,

and a storeroom for saddlery, and the armoury. These domestic quarters would
have been furnished with the discarded and broken furniture of previous generations. With the exception of rough and primitive tables in the kitchen, which
would also have had racks for meat and a simple cupboard for bowls and pots, the
furnishings would consist solely of the pallet beds or simple palliasses, a stool or
two, and a few rush-light holders.

The smaller country house. Smaller country houses, occupied either by gentry
of the standing of Chaucer's franklin, or by farmers or master weavers, were sometimes built on a more modest plan, a plan that would seem to have been that
generally used in the house of well-to-do but not wealthy merchants. The focal
centre of the house was again the hall, with the entrance in one of the long walls,
but without the interposition of a screen between the body of the hall and the
entrance, or with a screen with a central opening only. At one end, and forming
the main wall of the building, was the chimney-stack accommodating two fire-
places back to back, one serving the hall, the other the kitchen. Over the kitchen,
reached by a ladder or staircase, was the servant's bedroom. At the other end of
the hall and behind a boarded partition was the parlour, furnished in rather
different manner to the chamber of the same name in the larger country house.
It took on much of the character of the small bed-sitting room so frequently seen
in late medieval illuminations, which, in houses of the type under review, was also
used as a counting-house. The house being of only moderate size and of a limited
capacity, the parlour combined the functions of the parlour proper, the master's
bedroom, and his closet or place of business. The movables and immovables
therein would seem always to have been of the same character and number: a
canopied bedstead with a chest at the foot of it, a settle and "enclosed" table on
which the master worked at his accounts with the aid of counters, and against the
wall another settle or a built-in bench, with a hutch or aumbry upon legs, bearing
various pewter utensils. Above the parlour was a second bedroom.

The craftsman's house. In those domiciles in which some handicraft was
carried on, it was not unusual for the boarded end wall to be pierced high up with
a shuttered window overlooking the hall so that the work being done below might
be supervised. If the entrance was dignified with a porch, the floor above it
afforded space for a second room, frequently described today as an oratory; though
its most probable use was that of a closet. But such an addition called for the inser-
tion of a screen and would necessarily modify the entire arrangement of the interior. The hall itself, being half work-room, would be occupied with the looms or the
tools of the master's trade, and the domestic movables would be limited to the
master's chair, a stool for his wife, a table at which both family, workmen and
apprentices sat for meals upon forms, and a hutch and benches along the walls,
with perhaps a couple of chests beside a bed upstairs. Such a house would require

far less furniture both movable and immovable than a building of the type previously described. Yet it must not be supposed that such houses lacked good and substantial furnishings. There is a particularly apposite passage in William Harrison's *Description of England*, 1577, which hints vividly at the furnishing of a house of this type: "Manie farmers ... thinke his gaines verie small towards the end of his terme, if he have not six or seven yeares rent lieing by him, beside a fair garnish of pewter on his cupboard, with so much more in od vessels going about the house, three or foure feather beds, so many coverlids and carpets of tapestrie, a silver salve, a bowle for wine, and a dozen spoones to furnish up the sute".

The cottage. Architecturally and economically the cottage was a simplified and smaller version of the farmhouse on which it was modelled. It consisted of one moderately large room for living purposes, combining the functions of hall and kitchen, with a chimney-stack at one end housing a fireplace and oven, and a two-floored annexe, for sleeping accommodation and store-room: and the cottager's furniture was as simple as his home. Of what these movables consisted we can do little more than guess, since they have not survived. They met with the roughest usage, and when no longer serviceable were broken up for kindling. Nor are there any pictorial records of English cottage interiors of the time. The old illuminators of manuscripts, who, in the fourteenth century, delighted in portraying the daily doings of the peasantry, were no more. We must in our need then turn abroad for enlightenment, to Peter Brueghel the Elder and his brother interpreters of peasant life, whose permutations and combinations of the background essentials of the ever-recurring *Boors Carousing in an Inn* give us a reasonably accurate picture of a cottage interior at the period.

The cottager's main concern was for utility, and if his home was but barely furnished, it was because he lacked both the means to better it and the space therein to house anything more than necessities. A box-bed for the good-man and his wife; straw mattresses upon the floor for others in the household; a chest or two; some stools and a form; a rough table and a hutch for food; would be about as much in the way of movables that it would contain.

There is, however, an interesting passage in Warner's *The Patient Countess, c.* 1587, which shows that one convention at least of the great house was observed even in the humblest home, that which decreed that the master of the house should sit in a cushioned arm-chair at his board. The Countess's husband, with whose one amorous adventure the poem deals, is described as finding himself benighted at a "peakish graunge within a forest great". He is made welcome by the cottager and his wife, who regale him with their best provender – "browne bread, whig, bacon, curds and milk were set him on the borde". And for his ease – "A cushion made of lists, a stoole halfe backed with a hoope Were brought him, and he sitteth down beside a coupe".

There can be little doubt that this stool, with its hooped half-back, was the half-round chair which figures frequently in the representations of cottage life in the Middle Ages. The furnishings of the cottage would consist of wooden or basemetal spoons, wooden bowls and crocks for the storage of food, skillets and an iron or latten pot on a crane over the fire. Roast meat was the privilege of the manor house and the farm, while boiled meat was proper to the cottage. Scattered about would be the implements of husbandry, or those of the cotter's craft or trade.

Colour in sixteenth-century furniture. An entirely false impression of the appearance of the movables in the better-class house of the sixteenth century is conveyed by the present condition of so many pieces preserved either *in situ*, in museums or in private collections. Except in the cottages of the peasantry, furniture throughout the earlier Middle Ages was almost invariably painted, initially no doubt as a preservative. Manuscript illuminations, ecclesiastical sculptures and a few surviving pieces of furniture on the Continent afford ample evidences of this treatment during the twelfth, thirteenth and fourteenth centuries. There are authorities who maintain that this practice was still universal in the fifteenth century. It is evident that the carved decoration upon the legs of tables and upon bed-posts, based upon the heraldic chevron motif, was sometimes given added variety and emphasis by the use of colours and gilding applied over a gesso ground. Traces of original colour have been found in the undercutting of carving of many early pieces. But the practice of polychroming was not universal.

In the inventory recording the goods and chattels of Richard Tvocky, a well-to-do London grocer, drawn up in 1391, the hall of the house was furnished with the usual fixed wall benches – this may be deduced from the number of bankers and cushions listed – together with a large trestle table, a pair of tables of spruce – probably a chessboard – three forms and two chairs all unpainted, and "a painted table", probably the high table, and "a painted table for cups", a cup-board for the display of his plate. Illuminations depicting domestic interiors of the middle and second half of the fifteenth century very rarely show painted furniture. It was nearly always, even in the most exalted houses, of natural coloured wood. But with the 'thirties of the sixteenth century we find ample evidence of the return to favour of the use of colour on the domestic appointments. The Revels Accounts of this period show to what an extent colour was employed in important theatrical properties, provided by the Italian artist, Da Maiano, and the workmen of the Revels Office, for Hampton Court and the Palace of Placentia at Greenwich. Examples of such coloured work of about 1530 from Hampton Court are preserved in the Victoria and Albert Museum (*Guide* 1, No. 231). Thereafter the practice became general until, at the close of the century, upholstering in textiles replaced paint, and such pieces that were not so finished were just left with the surfaces wax polished.

The precise names of the movables and immovables in the foregoing summary afford the antiquary sufficient data on which to base a fairly accurate reconstruction of any room at the beginning, in the middle or at the end of the sixteenth century. In every form of applied art the period witnessed a more complete change than had ever happened before in England. In half a century, though the pattern of daily life did not alter to any marked extent, the trappings and accessories of that life underwent the amazing transformation implied by the substitution of the late renaissance ideals, designs and ornament for the Gothic. In that momentous half-century furniture completely changed in its outward appearance. Some movables disappeared from fashionable use, though individual pieces survived, to moulder away in kitchens, offices and stables. Others, though retaining their original names, were so modified in their construction that they are almost unrecognizable. Most of our present knowledge of the furniture of the sixteenth century is drawn from the wills and inventories of this period, and in them a constantly recurring vocabulary of terms for pieces of furniture is found. But the co-relation of these terms with existing sixteenth-century pieces in many instances presents a difficult problem.

The matter is still further complicated by the retention by contemporary writers of words, originally employed to describe particular movables, but later applied to others, which, though derived from the first, were entirely different from them both in form and function.

Moreover, names in common use among collectors and dealers today have in some instances only a recent history, and their sixteenth-century application was put to quite a different use. Others are purely romantic appellations invented in the nineteenth century. Much valuable work has been done in recent years in identifying types of furniture, but a rigid typology is impossible. The following pages are accordingly devoted to brief definite notices of the principal types of movables in use in the sixteenth century.

Aumbry. The earliest type of hutch for the storing of food or household necessaries now called a cupboard, was the aumbry or ambry. The aumbry began as the almery, whereby its purpose is indicated as a box in which to keep broken meats from the table, which were later to be given as alms to the needy and starving. Often it was a recess in the wall closed by a door, but it cannot have been long before the fixed aumbry, one of the immovables of the medieval household, was for convenience converted into a doored box which might be hung up or stood in any convenient position. In the sixteenth century the word aumbry was applied to any small hutch or doored receptacle built into a larger piece of furniture such as a cup-board, as for example in 1527 "a wainscot cupboard, with two aumbrys and two tills." However, in the early part of the century it is used equally with hutch for a large cupboard in the modern sense. One of the finest and most elaborate surviving example is that in the Burrell Collection. It has three doors, two above and one below, and two drawers or tills. A number of analogous pieces exist. There are two others in the Burrell Collection at Glasgow. The type seems to die out before the high middle of the century.

B

Beds. In the rooms in the private parts of the house the most important piece of furniture was the bed – whether of the post or boarded variety. During the sixteenth century both types, together with the truckle-bed, were in use. But their social standing was very different. The bed which in the later Middle Ages could have figured among the movables in the best room of a house of some distinction would have been of the usual stock type, a stout rectangular frame elevated on four legs, the sides and ends pierced with holes through which passed the cords which supported the mattress. It was quite unornamented, as it was draped with the bed-cover, and was normally quite hidden. Over it was suspended a tester or a rectangular framed canopy from which hung the bed-curtains, which at night could be drawn all round it to prevent draughts from reaching the occupant. During the day the curtains were drawn back so that the bed might be used as an extra seat, while the curtains at the foot were turned up and folded in upon themselves in such a way that they hung down like two swollen bags. Later a low panelled head was added.

The four-post bed which was *par excellence* the great bed of the sixteenth century had a similar bedstock, but the panelled tester was carried upon four posts, one at each corner. As the century advanced, the beds became larger and more elaborate, overburdened with ornament, caryatids and inlay. Some of the carving was enhanced with paint as in the illustration of the headboard of a bed in the possession of Mr L. G. G. Ramsey (Pl. 8).

In the late fifteenth and sixteenth centuries the type of bed usually found in poorer homes was the boarded bed. It was constructed in the fashion of a long open box with shallow sides, mounted on four legs. In this the straw mattress was laid. It was, however, a bed with an aristocratic ancestry, since in twelfth- and thirteenth-century illuminations it is shown as used by royalty, when the supports are usually represented as lions or fantastic monsters. By the sixteenth century, however, it had sunk in the social scale and was found only in farms and cottages, where it was no doubt regarded as the best bed, in the guest-rooms of inns of no great standing, and in the dormitories of the large residential schools. No examples of this early date are known to have survived. However, a print representing the dormitory of Westminster School included in the *Microcosm of London*, 1808, shows such beds still in use in the early nineteenth century. Each bed has a slightly elevated head provided with a narrow shelf on which a candle and books could be placed at need. And beds of exactly the same construction are still a feature of the dormitory of the Royal Hospital, Chelsea.

The truckle bed was, as its name indicates, a low bed or pallet upon truckles or solid wheels, which could be rolled out of sight under the great bed when not required. It was generally reserved for the use of a page or maid, who slept either in the master's or mistress's room or in the anteroom. They were still in use in palaces and the greater houses throughout the sixteenth century, but were not extensively in use in the average manor-house, which rarely possessed anterooms to the bedrooms. Those that survived were, like the box-bed, banished to the servants' quarters.

Chairs. Foremost among secular domestic chairs was the chair of estate, that which in gentle and noble houses was occupied by the master when he took his seat upon the dais in the hall behind the high table to preside at the daily assembling of his dependants at dinner. In houses other than palaces in the late fifteenth and early sixteenth centuries there was probably no more than one such chair, or two at the most, the second being of slightly lesser dimensions. The chair of estate like the table dormant was never moved from its commanding position

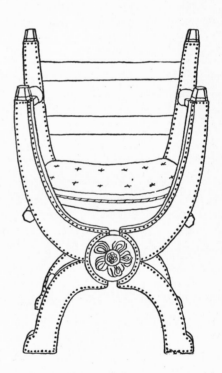

Fig. 1. "Joyned" chair of framed and panel construction; gothic in type. Early sixteenth century.

Fig. 2. Queen Mary's chair at Winchester Cathedral covered with blue velvet and garnished with gilt nails. The pommels and boss are copper gilt. *c.* 1550.

since, with the cloth of estate on the wall behind it, it was the visible symbol of the master. Its position was analogous to that of the throne in the throne-room of a palace. The earliest surviving English box-seated joined-chair is the Coronation

Chair in Westminster Abbey. This type of chair was the normal chair of estate of the late fifteenth and early sixteenth centuries. It is the chair which Randle Holme, the Chester Herald and antiquary, describes as "the settle chair ... having a kind of box or cupboard in the seat of it". (See *Academy of Armory*, 1688.) He adds, "being so weighty that it cannot be moved from place to place, but still in its owne Station". There is a fine example of about 1530 in the Victoria and Albert Museum (*Guide* 1, No. 328). An interesting variant, with a half-round panelled back, is in the Peter Gwynn Collection. This again, on account of its size and weight, must have occupied a fixed position. From inventories, however, we know that the parlour and master's bedroom also contained chairs, and examples of a more movable form, such as the so-called caqueteuse type, borrowed from France, were in vogue (Victoria and Albert Museum *Guide* 1, No. 327).

Another form of chair, of different origin from the boxchair, was the X chair. With a long history of royal and ecclesiastical use in palace and convent, it was a much more useful and movable object than the great wainscot chair, but much less able to stand rough usage. The earliest surviving English chairs of this fashion are those in York Minster and in Winchester Cathedral, the latter having been used at the marriage of Mary I to Philip of Spain in 1554 (Fig. 2). The other chair which must have been used at the same ceremony has never been traced.

Both chairs are assigned to about the same period – that is the middle of the sixteenth century – and there can be no doubt that this is correct of Queen Mary's chair. But there are excellent historical grounds for believing that the York chair is the best part of a century older, with which date nothing in its construction or ornament is at variance. It is illustrated in Henry Shaw's *Specimens of Ancient Furniture*, 1836.

By the second half of the sixteenth century the X chair must have become comparatively common, and this and other types of upholstered chairs appear in the houses of the wealthier gentry and of the more prosperous merchants. By then two modifications in the appearance of this chair and in its construction had taken place. The arms had in general ceased to be provided with pommels at their extremities, and were so shaped that the ends projected beyond the front uprights (Fig. 3), as in Sir Antonio Mor's portrait of Queen Mary, where the Queen is sitting in a chair of this fashion. Before the close of the century such chairs ceased to have seats formed of a squab cushion resting on the cradle of webbing, but were fully upholstered, the cushion being an integral part (Fig. 4). Late in the century we meet with a square joined-chair, the back of which is, however, clearly modelled on that of the X chair. A splendid example, formerly in the Duke of Buccleuch's Collection and now in Exeter Cathedral, is polychromed in green, gold and cream with trails of flowers and possesses some of its original green cut velvet upholstery. The "joyned" chair, the more usual type at the close of the sixteenth century, and which must have figured in most gentlemen's houses, carries the rectangular framing and scrolled arms carried by turned supports, with

the back decorated with the Elizabethan floral and chequered inlays, and surmounted by a scrolled cresting with brackets at either side. In lesser houses the
turned-chair, differing but little from its medieval prototype, continued in use.
Preserved in the President's Lodgings at Queens' College, Cambridge, is a very
beautifully proportioned and unique turned-chair, which tradition asserts, possibly correctly, was used by Erasmus during his residence at the University as Lady
Margaret Professor of Divinity. Two other chairs of turned work, but of a less
elaborate description, evidently intended for the use of schoolmasters of the sixteenth century, have survived at Westminster School.

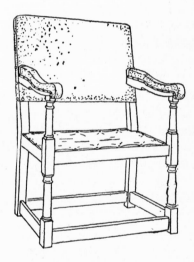

Fig. 3. An Elizabethan panelled chair
of transitional design between a box
seat and open frame.

Fig. 4. A late Elizabethan chair with a
beech frame. The back and the arms
are covered with velvet.

It has never been suggested that these turned, or, as they were usually known at
the period, "thrown" chairs were the products of one particular district. On the
other hand, the usually triangular-seated so-called "bobbin-frame chair", which
represents the frenzy of turnery, has no parallel on the Continent, and would seem
to have been confined to the Welsh Marches, the Severn Valley, and to Cheshire
and Lancashire. This type of chair in its embryonic form was unquestionably
known in the sixteenth century, though whether any of the more flamboyant
examples, such as that in the Victoria and Albert Museum, which in the *Guide* is

discreetly given to the sixteenth–seventeenth century, should be dated earlier than the beginning of the seventeenth century is doubtful. Until comparatively recently they were often ascribed to the reign of Henry VIII, an assumption based in all probability on the circumstance that one of the best-known examples of this type of chair was formerly preserved at Cheshunt Great House, where it was known traditionally as Cardinal Wolsey's Chair.

One type of arm-chair calls for particular notice, as its use was apparently confined to humble dwellings. On the evidence of illuminations it apparently consisted of a "half-compassed" seat supported on three narrow slab legs carrying a horse-shoe-shaped rail forming the back and arms. The space between the seat and the rail was usually filled with splats in the manner of a tub. On the evidence of other illuminations, unquestionably of English origin, the back was also made of a series of spindles passing at top and bottom into the rail and the seat, the interstices being filled with wicker-work. In some late examples that have survived the wicker-work is omitted.

Finally one particular variety of seat calls for passing notice. This is the so-called "monk's bench". The circumstance that the majority of the surviving examples are of the middle of the seventeenth century renders the phrase an obvious misnomer. Nevertheless, this bench-table, or chair-table, since some will hold only one sitter, has a very respectable ancestry, and a few examples are known of the turn of the fifteenth and sixteenth centuries.

Livery, court and close cup-boards. The cup-board, as the name implies, was the board upon which the cups – used loosely for all and any articles of plate which graced early dining-tables – were displayed in the hall for the envy and admiration of guests, when not in actual use. Such a display was not then thought of as ostentation. It was a gesture inspired by a wish to compliment an honoured guest. At ordinary times plate was securely locked away in chests and coffers. The unheralded visitor would be met by the sight of bare cup-boards, and his welcome would perhaps be limited to a friendly cup from the side-table, or a flagon from the livery hutch.

The cup-board itself in its early days was an open structure fitted with shelves, normally two or three one above the other, rising even to as many as six in the manner of that which, according to George Cavendish, graced Wolsey's Hall at Hampton Court – "cup-board ... of six desks high full of gilt plate, very sumptious". A similar arrangement may today be seen at Guildhall upon State occasions. Since, however, the cup-board in the hall was for use as well as for display, it was customary, long before the close of the fifteenth century, to enclose part of the space below the board with panels at the ends and doors in front, and in the resulting close cupboard or aumbry to store the extra napkins and kerchiefs of pleasaunce that might be required during dinner. These are clearly the "cup-boards with ambries" listed in the inventories of Henry VIII's furniture. Early examples of them can also be seen in the illuminations depicting domestic interiors which occur in manuscripts of the middle and second half of the fifteenth century. But it must be emphasized that the partial boxing-in of one or even two stages of the erection did not alter its nature: it still remained a cup-board (Pl. 4A).

No example of a sixteenth-century cup-board, *pur sang*, has yet been identified, and the difficulty of co-relating inventory entries with existing examples has been already mentioned.

Two constantly recurring types of cup-board are to be found throughout the second half of the sixteenth century. One type has two open stages or shelves with a pot-board below (Pls. 5, 6B). The other type is similar in appearance, but with an aumbry in the upper stage. The first type has been identified as a court cup-board, and the second as a livery cup-board, terms made familiar by their constant use in documents of the sixteenth century.

The phrase livery cup-board is partially self-explanatory, since here livery was clearly the daily allowance of food and drink provided for every member of the household. Some authorities maintain that it was so named from the circumstance that it was used as a resting-place for dishes and messes on the way from the kitchen to the table and from which they were taken to the diners. They have accordingly identified this particular form of cup-board with the open shelved type. Here it should be noted that certain cup-boards made for Hengrave Hall, Suffolk, in 1587–8 were to be "in the fashion of livery, that is without doors". Other authorities will have it that the livery cup-board was an enclosed or partly enclosed one in which that part of the livery not consumed at the tables – cold meats, cheese, butter, bread and ale – was kept until required for an informal collation such as supper or after-supper. In this connexion it is worth noting that livery cup-boards make a regular appearance among the furnishings of bedrooms. The close cup-boards were of similar form, but with the lower portion below the central shelf enclosed by doors.

Desks. More's closet at Loseley also included two desks, but there is no indication as to their exact nature. One or both may have been of the lectern type, the medieval *armariola*, with a lid inclined at an angle on which a book might be laid for reading. Actual examples are rare. There is a fine fifteenth-century desk of this type in the Victoria and Albert Museum (*Guide* 1, No. 320). Another is the famous standing desk from King Edward VI Grammar School, Stratford-on-Avon, now displayed at Shakespeare's birthplace. But desks of this type would appear more appropriate to an academic or pedagogic setting than to that furnished by the closet of a country gentleman. It is more probable that these two desks were table-desks, similar to that shown in Dürer's engraving of Erasmus, which, when boxed-in, became the desk-box, miscalled bible-box, of the seventeenth century.

Press. The term press, from its first recorded appearance in Chaucer's *Miller's*

Tale of 1386 – "His presse covered with a faldying reed" – would seem to have been used loosely to describe any tall, doored and shelved hutch used for storing napery, hangings or clothing. Like the word hutch-press, it was used in the sixteenth century to describe the small doored enclosure built into the upper stage of a cupboard, and in this sense it appears in a will made in Bury St Edmunds in 1552. The press proper, however, still maintained its pre-eminence as the largest type of hutch in the house, and when Master Ford (*Merry Wives of Windsor*, 1598, III iii, 226) is turning his house upside down in jealous fury at the Fat Knight, Sir Hugh Evans says that they have searched in the chambers, and in the coffers, and in the presses, the two last being the only pieces of furniture large enough to conceal a man. In the seventeenth century the press usually figures as the press cupboard – cupboard being used in its present sense – and in function it corresponded to the modern wardrobe (Pl. 7A).

Settles. Next to the spere or screen, the fixed bench was the most important of the immovables in the domicile of whatever description, and consisted in its most rudimentary form of a stout plank furnished at intervals along its fore or free edge with legs and braced at the back against the wall of the room. Other benches were affixed in the window recesses like modern window-seats. Still others were provided with backs and high ends. From this last developed the settle, which was merely a free standing bench that could be placed in any convenient position about the hall or chamber. The highbacked settle was a necessity in England, where screens to keep out draughts were unknown. In winter two or three grouped in strategic positions about the hearth made, when desired, a comfortable and cosy little room within the larger one. Settles of this nature continued to serve in farmhouses and in kitchens until well on in the nineteenth century.

Stools and Forms. All the stools that remain to us from the earlier part of the century are of the type of a fine example in the Burrell Collection, with solid end supports. Forms were of similar style and were sometimes made to match the tables they served. During the latter part of the century the four-legged joyned stool ousted the older type (Pl. 1B). These were sometimes made in matching sets. When not in use they were packed beneath the dining-table.

Close-stools. In More's inventory the close-stool or secret-stool is only once mentioned: "ij lettle close-stoles" are listed as in the children's chamber. The close-stool was a very necessary movable at a time when interior sanitation – at least in so far as the middle-class house was concerned – was in its infancy. In Tower Street, in the Parish of All Hallows, London – a street inhabited by wealthy merchants – it is recorded that in 1579 there were but three privies to meet the needs of near sixty houses. That great contemporary authority upon matters of health, Dr Andrew Boorde, urges that the common house of office of any domicile should be set over water or at the least at some distance from the house. We are, however, concerned more with close-stools than with jakes. An example which was at one time said to have belonged to Henry VIII is at Hampton Court. But upon examination it proves to be of a later age. Nevertheless the appearance, as in an example at Knole, probably approximates to that of the earlier article – a square box with a lifting lid covered with velvet held in place by gilded nails, and the top quilted for comfort.

Tables. In the first half of the sixteenth century, the principal table of the house and the position of its master's authority continued to be the medieval table dormant, the high table in the great hall. The trestle table was also still in use at Court. The secondary dining-tables for the servants and dependants may have also been fixed, or they may have been removable boards upon trestles after the old manner. But with the change of manners in the Elizabethan age and the decline of importance of the communal life of the great hall and the greater use of the private chambers, tables of another sort became the fashion. Draw-tables, where the board could be increased to almost double its length by the pulling out of the leaves below the top, were produced in large numbers, and though no doubt they were often used in the great hall, they were also to be found in the private chambers of the master and mistress. One of the earliest examples of the early part of the sixteenth century is the fine specimen in the Victoria and Albert Museum. But during the reign of Elizabeth they became very common. An unusual example in the Burrell Collection has the legs carved as figures instead of the more usual bulbs. An example with bulbs is in the Hart Collection (Pl. 3B).

Apart from the great tables in the hall, other lesser tables were scattered about the Tudor house and were used for various purposes, which can frequently be deduced from by their construction. In More's " chamber wherein I lye " is listed what was evidently an occasional table which, as already indicated, may have stood at his bed-head at night and served as a breakfast table in the morning. A second type of table is that which usually passes under the name of a "games table", a purpose which it may well have served. Like all free standing tables, they have all-round decoration. They are invariably furnished with a boxed upper section for the storage of dice, dice-boxes and the marked cloth that covered the table when in use. There is an interesting example at Penshurst; there are other examples in the Burrell Collection; and Mrs Hart's table here illustrated (Pl. 7B) is of exceptional character. The tops of these fold outward, and the legs are carved and stand upon stretcher feet in the fashion of the fifteenth century. All these tables, with the exception of Pl. 7B, are of the earlier part of the sixteenth century.

Hutch tables. There exists a class of table, of which about a score of examples are known, called, for want of a more scientific name, a hutch- or serving table. They have not so far been identified from inventories of the period, and take the form of a long, narrow side-table having a cupboard below, upon short legs. The top was often of the draw-type, but none with the original leaves *in situ* has yet been recorded. The best-known examples are those in the Victoria and Albert Museum and the collection of Lord Rochdale. A fine example in a private collection is illustrated (Pl. 1A). Some of the earlier examples evidently had tops which folded lengthways. The form is not found in later renaissance times; all the known examples are of the first half of the century.

One of the most celebrated and important from a documentary point of view is Sudbury's Hutch in St James' Church, Louth, Lincolnshire, though it has apparently undergone considerable restoration. The name is no piece of contrived archaism of the nineteenth century, since the phrase occurs in the churchwardens' accounts for 1586. The donor was one Thomas Sudbury, vicar of St James', whose incumbency began in 1451 and ended with his death in 1504. The hutch presumably originally stood in the hall of his Vicarage, as it is clearly domestic and is not an item of church furniture. It cannot antedate his death by many years, and its carved decoration proves that it was produced after Henry VII's accession in 1485. The principal motif is the Crowned Tudor Rose flanked by the heads of Henry VII and his queen, Elizabeth of York.

Turned ware. Before concluding the subject of domestic furniture of the sixteenth century something must be said of the productions of the wood-turners, generally known to collectors as "treen". The Worshipful Company of Turners of the City of London possess no records of an earlier date than the Grant of their Charter in 1604. But in 1478, though charterless, they were nevertheless an established and important manufacturing and trading association of craftsmen, and their ordinances were accordingly submitted to, and in that year approved by, the Court of Aldermen. These ordinances supply a too brief list of the wares which the turners produced – "shovels, scoopes, bushell trees, washing-bowls, chairs, wheels, pails, trays, truggers wares, wooden measures". Only a few of these were actually turned, and only half of them can be legitimately regarded as domestic utensils. At best the list must be regarded as a catalogue of headings, under each of which many kindred articles were included. Wash-bowls cannot have been the only type of bowl for which the Turners were responsible. Wooden bowls of various sizes had throughout the Middle Ages been almost the only tableware of the lower orders, the journeymen and apprentices in the towns and the peasants in the country districts. They were easy to make, their initial cost was negligible, and when solidly made they were almost indestructible. Small bowls replaced the cups of the wealthy classes, and larger ones held the stews of bacon or rabbit and vegetables that were the staple diet of the labouring classes. Mazer bowls appeared on the boards of both private houses and of charitable institutions and colleges, while large bowls were used for the storage of bread, milk, curds and cheese, and the like. Chairs must have implied not only the half-round and square-seated chairs previously noted, but stools of the type now generally referred to as "milking stools", together with the bases and uprights of spinning-wheels and embroidery frames and the frames of hour-glasses. The fact that the Turners produced pails and wooden measures shows that to some extent the Turners trespassed on the preserves of the Coopers. They must also have made cheese presses, of which the circular head of a very fine example incised with the arms of Edward IV is in the Strangers Hall at Norwich, together with a second one incised with the sacred monogram I.H.S., the latter being probably of the early sixteenth century. They must also have turned wooden trenchers, when these replaced trenchers of bread, and those charming painted roundles known to collectors as "fruit trenchers".

Horn. In leaving the subject of turnery it will be convenient here to add a few words on the contributions of the Horners to the way of life in the sixteenth century. In the Middle Ages the horn was still one of the principal drinking-vessels, as it had always been; and in parts of the country, in Wales particularly, the *Hirlas Horn* still remained until the seventeenth century the ceremonial vessel, a draught from which welcomed a stranger on arrival and sped his departure. But for all ordinary purposes it had been replaced by the cup and the bowl. The day of the horn tumbler was yet to come. But glass being beyond the reach of all but the very well-to-do, sheets of horn were inserted in window-frames and in the sides and fronts of lanterns. Horn spoons appeared upon the tables of the farm-house and the cottage. And in the days before the standish was known, or was at least a rarity, the turned ink-horn appeared on most desks, accompanied by the penner of tooled leather, horn or turned bone. These and other minor objects were not of great moment, but they were invaluable in an age and society that was debarred from using metal by its cost and had not achieved the blessings of this present age of plastics.

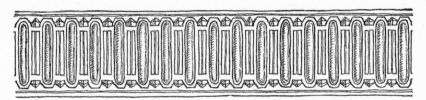

Fig. 5. Late Elizabethan carved gadroon ornament.

STUART

STYLISTICALLY, English seventeenth-century furniture falls into two main groups: first, joined furniture, which developed slowly on established lines from that in use during the Elizabethan period, comprising useful, solid, enduring articles, such as long tables, press cupboards, settles and joint stools, made usually of oak or indigenous woods; and secondly, post-Restoration furniture, the design of which was strongly influenced by contemporary models from France and Holland. This latter furniture, first made for the Court in London, resulted from the revolution in taste which followed the restoration of the monarchy in England in 1660. Some reaction against forms which had had their being under the Commonwealth was perhaps inevitable. There was a demand for luxury evidenced by the introduction of new specialized pieces, such as the scrutoir and bureau, dressing-glass and candle-stand. Fashionable post-Restoration furniture represented a break with tradition and was the work of new craftsmen, many of whom were Huguenot refugees, employing new techniques (veneering, marquetry, japanning and subsequently gesso) and new woods – in particular, walnut. Their productions were decorative and their standard of skill very much higher than that possessed by the native joiners. Their presence here was quickly felt. "Joyners, cabinet-makers, and the like ... from very vulgar and pitiful artists", wrote Evelyn, in a familiar passage, "are now come to produce works as curious for the fitting, and admirable for their dexterity in contriving, as any we meet with abroad."[1] Such furniture, however, was not in general supply under the late Stuarts. The provincial or country joiner was but little affected at this date by London fashions in furniture; he worked by usage and was incapable of making

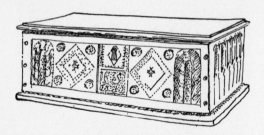

Fig. 6. Box of oak, with punch work ornament. Dated 1682.

[1] *An Account of Architects and Architecture*, by John Evelyn. *The Miscellaneous Writings of John Evelyn*, ed. by William Upcott, 1825, p. 361.

pieces other than those of familiar design and construction. Thus, much surviving furniture of late seventeenth-century date is in the style of the preceding period. Compare the oak box (Fig. 6), inscribed "I.S. 1682", decorated simply and in accordance with tradition, with punch work and gouge carving (at the ends), with a veneered walnut and marquetry counterpart of comparable date. The disparity of style and execution is remarkable.

A reliable account of the proper furnishing of a provincial gentleman's house in the late seventeenth century is provided by a contemporary writer, Randle Holme.[1] His *Academy of Armory*, published at Chester, contains definite instructions on this matter, as much else. The dining-room, he stated, is to be

well wanscoted about, either with Moontan[2] and panells or carved as the old fashion was; or else in larg square panell.

The Rome hung with pictures of all sorts, as History, Landskips, Fancyes, &c.

Lang table in the midle, either square to draw out in Leaves, or Long, or Round, or oval with falling leaves.

Side tables, or court cubberts, for cups and Glasses to drink in, Spoons, Sugar Box, Viall and Cruces for Viniger, Oyle and Mustard pot.

Cistern of Brass, Pewter, or Lead to set flagons of Beer, and Bottles of win in.

A Turky table couer, or carpett of cloth or Leather printed. Chaires and stooles of Turkey work,[3] Russia or calves Leather, cloth or stuffe, or of needlework. Or els made all of Joynt work or cane chaires.

Fire grate, fire shovell, Tongs, and Land Irons all adorned with Brass Bobbs and Buttons.

Flower potts, or Allabaster figures to adorn the windows, and glass well painted and a larg seeing Glass at the higher end of the Rome.

Holme's list of items, printed at a time when new building and the "politer way of living" had already exercised a great effect on furniture styles, is informative. He was prepared, seemingly, to compromise between the claims of old and new fashions and to allow considerable freedom of choice to the householder.

I. FURNITURE OF PRE-RESTORATION CHARACTER

The great houses: the Lumley inventories. Surprisingly few varieties of domestic furniture existed in England at the beginning of the century, even in the richest houses. This is sufficiently clear from the inventory of the possessions of John, Lord Lumley, taken by his steward of household, one John Lambton, in 1590.[4] The inventory is of considerable length and details the "monumentes of Marbles, Pictures and tables in Paynture, with other ... howseholde stuffe and

---

[1] *The Academy of Armory, or, a Storehouse of Armory and Blazon*, by Randle Holme, Chester, 1688. Roxburghe Club edit., 1905, Vol. II, pp. 15–16. The MS. is dated 1649, when Holme completed his "first collection and draughts" for the work.

[2] *Mountan* or *Muntin*. A vertical member of the framing of wainscot or other panelled woodwork.

[3] A coarse wool needlework, made in imitation of a Turkey carpet.

[4] *The Lumley Inventories* by Lionel Cust, and *A Lumley Inventory of 1609* by Mary F. S. Hervey, *Walpole Society*, Vol. VI, 1917–18, pp. 15–35, 36–46.

Regester of Bookes" at Lord Lumley's three houses – Nonesuch Palace, the London house on Tower Hill, and Lumley Castle. The pictures may here be disregarded, as also the statuary. The fantastic marble objects (tables, screens, and fountains), which are recorded by the several pages of drawings prefacing the inventory, have not survived. (It is likely that these pieces were the work of Italian craftsmen.) A table, now at Aston Hall, Birmingham, with polychrome marble top inlaid in an elaborate perspective design, is, however, representative of this small but fashionable class of Italian or Italianate furniture; the table is certainly of Italian inspiration, although its square wooden frame, carved with strapwork

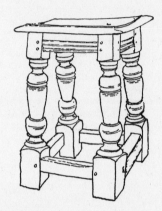

Fig. 7. Painted arm-chair, made probably from the design of Francis Cleyn, after an Italian model. Height 3 ft. 7½ in. *c.* 1625.

Fig. 8. Oak "joint" stool; the seat has a moulded edge and is supported on turned legs united by plain stretchers. Height 1 ft. 9 in. Mid-seventeenth century.

decoration, is English work of about 1600. The unusual and interesting chair reproduced in Fig. 7 is, too, strongly Italian in style. There is good reason to suppose that it was made to the design of the elder Francis Cleyn,[1] master of the tapestry works for Charles I at Mortlake. Cleyn is known to have been in Italy for some four years. The chair is almost identical with those "carved and gilt, with large shells for backs" which were noted by Horace Walpole as being in a room decorated by Cleyn at Holland House, and remarked as being "undoubtedly from his designs, and evidences of his taste".[2]

It is difficult now to conceive a true idea of the splendid character of the furnishing of the rooms of these houses: their brilliance derived largely from valuable fabrics, and gold and silver plate. Many "sutes of hanginges of arras, sylke and

[1] Francis Cleyn was born at Rostock in 1582. He studied in Rome and Venice. Court Painter to Christian IV of Denmark. Cleyn was in England from 1625, and died in London, 1657–58.

[2] *Anecdotes of Painting in England*, by Horace Walpole; 1st. edit. Strawberry Hill, 1762–71. See *English Decoration and Furniture of the Early Renaissance*, by Margaret Jourdain, 1924, wherein C. J. Richardson's lithographs of Holland House are reproduced, Figs. 16, 127, and *The Baronial Halls . . . of England*, by S. C. Hall, F.S.A., 1858, Vol. I, p. 7.

tapistre" (fifty-seven), "Turkye carpettes of sylke" (eleven) and "other Turky Carpettes" (ninety-five) were listed in the Lumley inventory, with "carpettes of velvet for tables and wyndowes" (twenty-five) and "coveringes and Quyltes of sylke" (forty). There were "quisshins [cushions] of clothe of gold, velvet and sylke" (one hundred and nine); indeed many chairs (seventy-six) and stools (eighty) were covered with these materials, and a few with red Spanish leather, or with crewel needlework. The essential wooden, and un-upholstered, furniture by comparison showed small variety and comprised only chairs (seventeen), stools (one hundred and seventy-five), forms (twenty), tables (seventy-five) and cupboards (fifty-two), which were distinguished as of "walnuttre and Markatre" (walnut decorated with an inlay of woods), of "walnuttre" and of "Waynskot" (imported oak). Oak furniture, of course, preponderated over walnut, but not to the extent that was general in most houses. Bedsteads were "gylt" (four), "of walnuttre and markatre" (twenty-three) and "of weynskot" (forty), and there were, besides, the "pallet beddes with their bolsters" and "lyvereye beddes" which were in common use. Curiously, there is no mention of the chests, which must have been numerous; they were not here valued.

A second Lumley inventory taken for probate in 1609 ("a trew Inventarie of all such moveables as were found in Lumley Castle after the decease of the Lord John Lumley ...") is as to furniture more explicit. We have such entries as these: "Itm two long drawinge [draw] tables of walnottree one folding table of wainscott & a little table of wainscott"; "Itm two fyne merketree cupboards & two livere cupbords"; Itm x square oake & elme tables & liverie Cupbords sutable"; and "Itm one old iron chist & a firre chist". This inventory applies only to Lumley Castle; consequently the number of entries contained in it is greatly reduced.

Upholstered seat furniture. Upholstered seat furniture of a luxurious character existed in quantity by the early seventeenth century in many of the great houses of England. This furniture, because of its perishable nature, has almost entirely disappeared. (Knole, Kent, where early upholstered chairs, stools, and couches remain still in untouched condition, if sadly worn and faded, provides a notable exception.)[1] The 1590 inventory, it may be noticed, listed as many as seventy-six "Chares of Clothe of gold, velvet and sylke" but seventeen only "of walnuttre and markattre" (i.e. joined chairs, see below).

These chairs, which were the products of the upholsterer,[2] were in general "covered all over" (i.e. all exposed surfaces were covered with fabric), "garnished with nails", and "fringed with gold". They were constructed with frames of beechwood – a wood particularly liable to attack by worm. It is probable that numerous

---

[1] See *The Upholstered Furniture at Knole*, by R. W. Symonds, *The Burlington Magazine*, May and July 1945. The illustrations include a chair of early X-shape design, one of rectangular form with low stuffed back, and couches.

[2] And, at first, of the coffer maker.

suites of upholstered seat furniture were made under the early Stuarts, comprising chairs, couches and stools. At this time the single chair, or "back-stool", with stuffed seat and back first emerges. The low-backed farthingale chair, said to have been designed to accommodate ladies wearing the farthingale, which attained extravagant proportions under James I, was also made without arms and is distinguished by a wide and very high, stuffed seat (Pl. 11A). It was supported usually on columnar legs and covered frequently in "Turkey work".

Comparatively few upholstered stools have survived, although they would seem once to have been plentiful. According to Sir John Harington, writing in the later sixteenth century, upholstered stools were to be seen "in every merchant's hall". Indeed, men could "scant endewr to sitt upon" the hard plank forms and wainscot stools "since great breeches were layd aside".[1]

At the time of the Commonwealth, leather coverings were introduced; strips of hide were strained over seat and back panel and secured by large brass-headed nails.

Joined chairs, stools and benches. Joined chairs are listed in most early seventeenth century inventories, and evidently were owned by all but the poorest sections of the population. They were not numerous, at least in the houses of yeomen and country tradesmen, and were reserved for the master of the house and his guests. John Osburne, for example, a yeoman of Writtle, in Essex, whose goods and chattels were appraised in 1638, kept: "In the Hall – one great ioyned table, eigght stooles and one forme, 1 *li*. 10*s*.; one litle ioyned table, 2 stooles and one great ioyned chayer, 8*s*.; one cubbard & one settle with 3 boxes in it, 1 *li*." While Robert Jackson, also of Writtle, the inventory of whose goods was taken that same year, possessed: "In the Hall One table, 2 formes, one Joyned stole, 1 *li*. 6*s*. 8*d*.; 2 little tables, 2 chayres, 8*s*.; 1 bench bord, 4 cushens ... 13*s*.;" and, "In the Porler – One Joyned bedsted with all that belongeth to it, 5 *li*.; 2 chayers, 1 little table and one Joyned stole, 1 Cuberd, one warming pan, 1 *li*. 15*s*."[2]

At the beginning of the century, joined chairs with open arms and panel backs were still of very substantial construction. They were at that time rarely made of walnut. Ordinarily, the back panels were arched and, in some finer specimens, decorated with a floral inlay. Such inlay was of holly, bog oak, box, yew, the fruitwoods and other woods, such as ash and poplar. The legs were baluster turned or of columnar form, and tied by moulded stretchers.[3] Chairs tended to be more lightly made as the century advanced. Certain stylistic changes may be remarked: first, in later chairs, the downward slope of the arms is more pronounced; secondly

---

[1] *Nugae Antiquae*: being a collection of original papers in prose and verse by Sir J. H. and others, 1804 edit., Vol. I, p. 202.

[2] *Farm and Cottage Inventories of mid-Essex*, 1635–1749, ed. by F. W. Steer, 1950.

[3] See *The Dictionary of English Furniture*, revised edition by Ralph Edwards, 1954, Vol. I, p. 231 – *Chairs*, Figs. 18, 19 and 21.

the top rail of the chair back (which bears a scrolled cresting) later often rests on the uprights, and is not contained within them, and pendant brackets, or "ear-pieces", are attached at the sides, below the cresting; and, finally, the thin wooden seat, conforming to a lighter pattern of chair, is narrower (Pl. 12B). In many post-Restoration chairs of this panel back type the decorative area of the back is thinly but profusely carved with strapwork, scrolls or floral arabesques. Such features as the foregoing provide some indication of the date of construction. But panel back chairs were supplied to farmhouses and cottages at least until the middle of the eighteenth century; and modifications in their design made over many years in any one locality were often slight. The variety to be found in surviving chairs is due in large part to the stylistic differences which existed between the furniture of one region and another. The carved oak single chair, dated 1641, which is illustrated in Pl. 11B, is, for example, from the north country. The influence of region on furniture style was considerable.

Joined stools and benches were in common use as seats, particularly at the dining-table, and innumerable sets of stools, and benches, were made; they were often "sutable" (i.e., designed *en suite*) to the table. (Stools were ranged under the table when not in use, and rested on its stretcher rails.) Stools, like chairs, deve-loped towards lightness, and the somewhat massive carved and fluted legs found in late Elizabethan examples, were, too, succeeded by those of columnar or turned baluster form. These supports were slightly splayed, so as to give stability to the seats (Fig. 8). Three-legged or "cornered" joined stools were also made. Benches and forms, less used in the seventeenth century, developed on similar lines, being, by construction, no more than heavy elongated stools, purposed to seat several persons.

Settles. Settles resembled in form contemporary chairs, but were made with very high backs. They were either movable or fixed; and were extremely popular pieces, particularly in poorer households, where they offered comparative comfort as seats, both by virtue of a position by the fireside and as providing protection against draughts. Most late settles, supplied to farmhouses and cottages, were of a serviceable and composite nature. In many, a locker was contained beneath the seat, which was hinged and opened as the lid of a chest. Some settles, construc-ted with a hinged back, combined the functions of seat and table (Pl. 12A).

Cupboards. Cupboards figure prominently in inventories of the period, but seldom are particularized. But while it is clear that cupboards of several types existed in most houses of substance, and were to be found in hall, parlour and bed-rooms, it is yet difficult exactly to identify the purpose served by many of the numerous surviving specimens.[1]

The court-cupboard, introduced by the third quarter of the sixteenth century,

[1] See Edwards, *op. cit.*, Vol. II, pp. 156 ff.

C

or earlier, and possessed by manors and the larger farmhouses by about 1600, had, however, a definite place in the dining parlour and was used for the display of plate and as a service table. (Those which were made under Elizabeth and James I were often of walnut and were richly carved and inlaid, as befitted ceremonial pieces.) The function of the court-cupboard remained the same throughout the course of the century. It was specifically listed by Randle Holme[1] in his work of

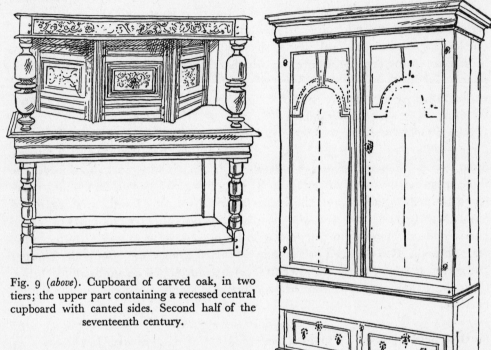

Fig. 9 (*above*). Cupboard of carved oak, in two tiers; the upper part containing a recessed central cupboard with canted sides. Second half of the seventeenth century.

Fig. 10 (*right*). Clothes-press of walnut; door, drawer fronts and sides veneered and decorated with herring-bone inlay and cross-banding. Height 6 ft. 7 in. Early eighteenth century.

1688, as being among those "things necessary for and belonging to a dineing Rome". The court cupboard was of open construction, in three tiers, and rarely exceeded 3 ft. 10 in. in height. The tiers were supported at front, at the corners, usually by bulbous columns. These were a distinctive feature, and were at first of pronounced "cup and cover" form, but later modified and attenuated, and, towards the end of the century, undefined, except sometimes by grooving. Drawers were contained behind the upper and middle friezes, and "carpets" or cloths were laid on the shelves. The late court-cupboard, particularly after 1700, is usually of comparatively poor quality, the design stinted, and the character of the carved

[1] See Holme, *op. cit.*, Vol. II, p. 15.

decoration inferior. It was at that time the unfashionable product of the country joiner, and had been superseded by the side table.

Two other types of cupboard, related closely structurally to the open court-cupboard, but each formed with an enclosed upper stage, were also in common use. First, a splay-fronted cupboard, with central door, which presumably served much the same purpose as an open "cup-board" (there is adequate room for the display of "flaggons, cans, cups, and beakers" on the shelves) and may also have been described as a "court cupboard". Its dimensions are much the same; and often both friezes open as drawers. And, secondly, a straight-fronted cupboard enclosed by a door or doors above and flanked by panels, which, although of similar proportions to the court-cupboard, must be regarded as a piece distinct from it, more akin to the press. An example of the former type, dating from the second half of the seventeenth century, is illustrated in Fig. 9. Here, bulbous columns in front have given way to vase-shaped and squat baluster turned supports. The flat posts at the back corners are standard as, too, is the moulded edge to the central shelf. The carving, decorating the upper frieze and bordering the panels of the front of the enclosed stage below, is shallow and recessed – another late feature. Sunk or recessed carving was much employed on post-Restoration provincial oak furniture, and was utilized by the country joiner as a comparatively easy method of carving. Often, the ground was punched, so as to throw the design into relief.

The press or "close" cupboard was to be found throughout the century in the living-rooms and bedrooms of most houses, large and small. The press was an extremely useful piece of furniture, and plain specimens of oak or a native wood were made in country districts well into the eighteenth century. Many late presses are dated. In some, the upper stage was recessed; the frieze was supported by turned bulbous columns (which were later replaced by pendant bosses) framing the upper doors and resting on a narrow shelf (Pl. 9B). The large cupboard doors of a substantial lower stage were often divided into one horizontal panel with two vertical panels below. Other presses, with a plain front, and fitted with shelves, were designed for use in the bedrooms, or as storage pieces. There survive also a number of interesting specimens which were made with cupboard doors and drawers in the lower portion; the combination was not unusual (Pl. 9A). In general presses were between 5 and 6 ft. high, and tended to develop towards greater width. They were not fashionable by the late Stuart period, and it is significant that few walnut or marquetry examples have survived (but see Fig. 10). Three-tiered cupboards – distinctive in appearance and of Welsh origin – are known as *tridarns*.

Small hanging cupboards, for food, enclosed by doors each with one or more open rows of turned spindles, which provide the means of ventilation, date for the most part from the first half of the century (Pl. 10B). Later examples are more roughly made, but sometimes still very decorative.

Long tables. The long framed tables and draw tables of this period were substantially made; and were, by Evelyn's phrase, "as fixed as the freehold", intended to endure and give service to many generations. They were used for dining, and were to be found in hall and parlour; and they have survived in large numbers, often in good condition. Some smaller varieties of table, however, which are listed in most contemporary inventories, and which must have been plentiful from an early date (since they would be required for many different purposes), are comparatively scarce. Indeed, a "square table", of which there is frequent enough mention, is not certainly to be identified with a known existing type. Small round and oval tables, and tables with octagonal or polygonal tops, of sixteenth-century date, are known, and specimens are often of very decorative appearance, with an elaborately arcaded underframing. Many tables were constructed with a folding half-top and some form of gate support, and from these latter derived the small gate-leg tables with hinged flaps ("falling" tables), made in increasing numbers, and size, under the Stuarts (see **Gate-leg tables** below).

Most of the long framed tables of seventeenth-century date which remain are of oak or, less commonly, of elm or yew; walnut was rarely used at this period. During the reign of James I these tables were supported on columnar legs or on massive carved legs of an exaggerated bulbous form, and were tied by moulded stretchers. The supports are a distinctive feature. The bulb, Flemish or German in origin, built up from several sections and sometimes ornately carved with acanthus and gadroons was of a well-defined "cup and cover" form, with an ionic capital above a thin turned neck. The bulb became much modified in the course of the first half of the century. Some later tables had a graceful vase turned leg, but a coarse form of turning (reminiscent of bobbin turning) was to be found in many of those made during the Commonwealth, or the period immediately succeeding.

Tables were frequently of great length, and many of those with fixed tops had six or eight legs and intermediate cross stretchers. Draw tables, however, which were fitted with two subsidiary leaves (attached to raking bearers and situated under the main board), and might be extended to almost double their length, were supported only at the four corners.[1] Their height, when closed, was generally about 2 ft. 9 in. Draw tables and long tables with fixed tops were made contemporaneously and their stylistic development followed a parallel course.

A draw table now at the Oak House Museum, at West Bromwich (Pl. 10C), is a good late specimen and, characteristically, is simple in design, with a minimum of carved decoration. The frieze, which in many earlier tables dating from the first third of the century was noticeably used as a field for a decoration of inlay, often of chequer pattern, or was elaborately carved with strapwork, with flutings, gadroons or lunettes, is here plain. The bulbous supports of the table are much attenuated and their "cup and cover" form is barely defined by a carved grooving. There are

---

[1] See Edwards, *op. cit.*, Vol. II, p. 130 – *Construction*, Fig. 7.

ring mouldings above and below the bulbs. The top consists of two narrow boards, set in a mitred surround. The length of the table, unextended, is 6 ft. 9 in.; and with both end leaves fully drawn out, 11 ft. 6 in. As is so often the case with these tables, the feet, which finished in square blocks, have been cut by some 2 or 3 in. The table stands now at 2 ft. 7 in.

Long tables with fixed tops, the friezes of which are decorated on one long side only, clearly were designed for use as side or serving tables. Tables of trestle construction, which were still made in the seventeenth century, may have been put to the same use.

Gate-leg tables. Gate-leg tables are among the most useful and pleasing pieces of seventeenth-century furniture readily to be acquired by the collector. Tables of this class have survived in surprisingly great variety, and are dissimilar in construction, size and shape, and in the character of supports and stretchers. Gate-leg tables when extended were round, oval, square, oblong or polygonal; and the number of supports ranged from three to twelve. They were joined by mortice and tenon, secured by dowel-pins. Most of these tables were made in the post-Restoration period, when the habit of dining at separate small tables became fashionable, and when a very considerable demand existed.

The early type of gate-leg table (a "folding" table) was of semi-circular form, with a single gate. It was designed to stand against a wall when closed, and was supported on three legs tied by a semi-circular stretcher. One of the two back legs was halved vertically and framed to the stretcher (also halved) so as to form a single swinging gate. The table when open was circular and was then supported at four points. In other types with hinged double tops, the gate was formed as a complete section. Tables with a triangular framing and a semi-circular overhanging top were often constructed with four legs, one of which was attached to the gate, and was movable. A number of tables of this sort, with a triangular top (which opened to a square form), were intended to stand in the corner of a room. This is evident from the fact that the side to which the gate was attached, and the gate itself, frequently was decorated with carving. Tables of polygonal form were often provided with four fixed supports, in addition to those of the movable gate. The "folding" table, with carved and arcaded underframing and gate supported on a ground shelf, which is shown in Pl. 10A, is of this description. The character of the decoration, in particular the applied ornament, suggests that the piece dates from the middle years of the century.

Oval tables with "falling" tops and a gate on either side made their appearance early in the century. The centre portion of these tables was fixed, and usually was supported either by solid trestle uprights pegged into a base-board at each end, or by turned balusters, finishing in trestle feet, tied by a double stretcher, or by turned legs at each of the four corners (Pl. 15). The last type is that most commonly to be seen. The legs on either side, four in number, two of which compose the gate, were baluster turned or twist turned, and the stretchers, square or turned; the hinged flaps of the fixed top were upheld by the gates. Often a drawer was fitted in the underframing. Some of these tables which were made after the Restoration were of exceptional size (between 7 and 8 ft. long) and provided with four gates; they were therefore furnished with twelve legs. However, these tables did not provide a satisfactory solution to the problem of seating a large number of people at one table, because of the lack of leg room, and consequently few were made; but they are very handsome pieces of furniture. Occasionally they were made with square tops.

An ingenious and singularly attractive type of small gate-leg table, with a single pivoting gate, so constructed as to uphold both flaps, was also made.[1]

Gate-leg tables were generally of oak, particularly the larger specimens, but yew and the fruitwoods were employed with good effect by country craftsmen. Walnut is found used in some tables made after the Restoration.

Beds. The Elizabethan and early Stuart great bed was of very substantial proportions. The panelled headboard, usually of architectural character, with arcaded decoration and pilasters sometimes in the form of terminal figures, was elaborately carved and inlaid with floral ornament. The massive bulbous foot-posts, supported on pedestals of square section, were free standing (i.e. were clear of the bedstock), and served to carry a heavy, panelled tester. The hangings were of velvet or other rich materials. Beds of this type were of considerable consequence and were handed down from one generation to the next.

"Joined" beds figure largely in inventories of the time. They are not in general to be identified with the great beds of the foregoing description, but rather with beds of box-form, with panelled head, foot and canopy, which in construction resemble those made at the same time on the Continent (many, presumably, were fitted with enclosing side curtains); or with the low "stump" beds, of panelled construction, with short corner-posts and an open foot which were in common use, and which continued to be made throughout the seventeenth and eighteenth centuries.

Chests. The very numerous chests made throughout this century were mostly of framed and panelled construction. "Boarded" chests (i.e. chests wherein the solid front is rebated into the ends, which form the supports) were comparatively rare.

Many early seventeenth-century chests were decorated with a floral inlay used in combination with carved ornament. Some specimens were arcaded in front, the stiles framing the arches being carved with conventional ornament, or, occasionally, faced with terminal figures. An all over decoration of carving in low relief is often found in chests dating from the second quarter of the century, particularly those coming from northern and eastern districts (Pl. 11c).

[1] See Edwards, *op. cit.*, Vol. III, p. 239 – *Tables, gate-leg*, Fig. 20.

2. THE POST-RESTORATION STYLE

Veneered cabinet furniture. From the reign of Charles II, new methods and materials were largely employed in the making of cabinet furniture. The period from the Restoration to the reign of George I is distinguished by an extensive use of walnut, both in the solid and as a veneer. *Juglans regia*, the English variety, pale brown in colour, with brown and black veining, and *Juglans nigra*, the "black wood", which resembles mahogany, were both being grown in England by the later seventeenth century, but in insufficient quantity to meet the increased demand. "Were the timber in greater plenty amongst us", remarked Evelyn, "we should have far better utensils of all sorts for our Houses, as chairs, stools, Bedsteads, Tables, Wainscot, Cabinets, etc., instead of the more vulgar beech, subject to the worm, weak and unsightly: – I say if we had store of this material we should find an incredible improvement in the more stable furniture of our houses."[1] The scarcity of walnut was met in part by importations from the Continent (especially from France) and from Virginia, and by the use of other decorative woods such as olive ("highly in request" as a veneer), laburnum and kingwood (then described as "princes wood"). The cuts of these woods possessed the variety and richness of figure desired by the veneerer.

Veneering "whereby several thin slices or leaves of fine wood of different sorts are applied and fastened on a ground of common wood",[2] hitherto had been practised to a very limited extent in England. From the Restoration, however, veneered furniture, inspired by foreign example and workmen, became fashionable. Veneered work was the product of a cabinet maker. Veneers were laid by means of glue on the flush prepared surfaces of a carcase wood. Panel construction, long employed by the joiner, was by this technique in the main discarded. Joiners, of course, and craftsmen in the country, continued to make pieces in "wainscot", that is in imported oak; and some attempted to adapt their designs to new fashions. And "wainscot furniture", of joined construction and unveneered, was cheaper and popularly supplied to all classes throughout the "Walnut period".

Equally, many of those workmen employing new styles and techniques were dependent to a greater or lesser degree on tradition. The walnut clothes-press (Fig. 10), a rare and interesting piece dating from the early eighteenth century (the design of its cornice and convex frieze is characteristic, and is found on the veneered walnut and marquetry "scrutoirs" fashionable under the late Stuarts), illustrates the complexity and variety of production throughout the period. Compare this piece with the oak press of framed construction (Pl. 9A).

Lacquer and japanning. Soon after 1660, oriental lacquer furniture was imported in quantity by the East India Company, and offered for sale in many of the

---

[1] *Sylva*, by John Evelyn, 1664.   [2] *New and Universal Dictionary of Arts and Sciences*, 1756.

"curiosity" shops at that time existing in London. Oriental lacquer was of two varieties: incised lacquer, known as "Bantam work", which was shipped in the form of screens, or plain boards, often subsequently made up into mirror frames (Pl. 17A), table-tops or cabinets, sometimes with curious effect;[1] and a lacquer with raised gilt ornament on a hard, smooth, polished ground, in colour generally black. (The numerous lacquer cabinets of late seventeenth-century date, and later,

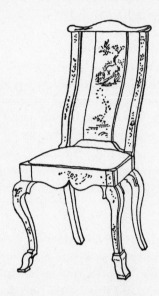

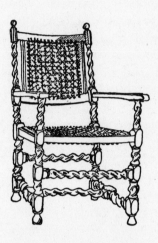

Fig. 11. Chair of beech-wood, japanned green and gold on a red ground. Height 3 ft. 9 in. Early eighteenth century.

Fig. 12. Arm-chair of turned walnut with caned back and seat. c. 1665.

which have survived are of this latter sort; they were mounted on decorative carved and gilt stands of English manufacture.) By the 1680's the "Indian" wares, as they were called, were being very commonly imitated in England, both by professional workmen and by amateur decorators, and a *Treatise of Japaning and Varnishing* produced by John Stalker and George Parker in 1688, which gave instruction in the art, enjoyed a considerable success. Certainly, the directions given by the authors of this work are technically sound and would seem to have been followed closely by contemporaries. The European imitations of oriental lacquer (see Pl. 17B and Fig. 11) properly are to be termed "Japan" rather than

[1] The mirror frame (Pl. 17A) was carelessly constructed, and illustrates the contemporary statement that "Bantam work" was "obsolete, and out of fashion . . . no person fond of it . . . except some who have made new Cabinets out of old Skreens. And from that large old piece, by the help of a Joyner, made little ones . . . torn and hacked to joint a new fancie . . . the finest hodgpodg and medly of Men and Trees turned topsie turvie." *A Treatise of Japaning and Varnishing* . . . (1688) by J. Stalker and G. Parker.

"lacquer" and were produced by a method which was akin to varnishing.[1] This distinction, however, was not observed in the seventeenth century; the term "Japann" was then applied indiscriminately to furniture of Eastern origin or home manufacture.

Gesso. Gilt furniture enjoyed considerable popularity at this period. The fashion for gilding first appears under Charles II in the many floridly carved and gilt stands which were made for imported oriental cabinets, and in elaborately decorative side-tables, mirrors and stands dating from late Stuart times. These latter are magnificent pieces, strongly influenced by French models.

Gesso furniture, which may be regarded as a subsidiary branch of gilt furniture, is found in England after about 1690. The technique is distinctive. Gesso ornament is executed in very low relief and follows the lines of an intricate and symmetrical traced pattern, usually "arabesque" in nature. The gesso, a composition of chalk and parchment size, was applied in successive thin coats to the surface (already roughly carved) of the piece to be decorated, and when hardened was re-carved, sanded or punched, and gilded. Gesso was most suitable for the decoration of large flat surfaces, such as table-tops (Pl. 13). During the reign of Anne, gilt gesso was frequently applied to the mirror frame.

Marquetry. Furniture of "markatre" is recorded in numerous inventories of early seventeenth-century date. The term "markatre" then was descriptive of inlaid furniture. Marquetry, however, as we now know it, was not introduced into England from the Continent until shortly after the Restoration. (Evelyn, in *Sylva*, which was first published in 1664, refers to certain exotic woods used in marquetry decoration.) The technique was distinct from that of inlay, and comparable with veneering. Small veneers of different coloured woods, cut to various shapes, were assembled, according to a prepared design, and set in a veneer ground. This composite veneer overlaid the carcase wood. Patterns were usually floral, or of flowers with birds, and at first were brightly coloured. Certain of the woods used for the patterns (these included fruitwoods, yew, beech, holly or sycamore) were stained. The marquetry decoration was in many cases reserved in panels, usually oval in shape.

"Seaweed" or arabesque marquetry, which was a later development, particularly fashionable in the first years of the eighteenth century, was conceived on a smaller scale and was subdued in colouring. The delicate and intricate scrolling patterns were executed in two woods only – box, or sometimes holly, on a walnut ground. In the character of the decoration the influence of André Charles Boulle and other French artists working under Louis XIV is clearly discernible. The woods of the pattern and the ground were sometimes reversed, as in the *partie* and

---

[1] Japanning consists in "covering bodies by grounds of opake colours in varnish; which may be either afterwards decorated by painting or gilding, or left in a plain state. . ." (Robert Dossie, 1758).

contre partie of Boulle. "Seaweed" marquetry was used sometimes in conjunction with parquetry.

Many of the small walnut tables with twist – or baluster-turned legs which came into favour after the Restoration were decorated with marquetry. The "little table with a drawer" illustrated in Pl. 14 is characteristic in design of this type. The panels of arabesque marquetry of the table top are bordered by broad bands of oyster-shell veneer; and the supports are tied by a flat stretcher with Y-shaped ends connected by an oval platform. The stretcher, like the edge of the top, is veneered in cross-banded walnut.

Cane furniture. Cane chairs first were produced in England early in Charles II's reign, as is evident from the wording of a petition to Parliament by the cane-chair makers in the 1680's, wherein it was stated:

> . . . That about the Year 1664, Cane-Chairs, &c. came into use in *England*, which gave so much Satisfaction to all the Nobility, Gentry, and Commonalty of this Kingdom, (for their Durableness, Lightness, and Cleanness from Dust, Worms and Moths, which inseparably attend Turky-work, Serge, and other Stuff-Chairs and Couches, to the spoiling of them and all Furniture near them) that they came to be much used in *England*, and sent to all parts of the World. . .[1]

The early examples resembled in form, if not in materials, leather covered chairs in use under the Commonwealth; and indeed for some years the two types were produced contemporaneously. The low square back, set rather high above the seat rail, and the seat itself, were filled with a coarse-meshed caning; the legs, uprights and stretcher rails were twist turned; and the arms were flat, very slightly shaped, and horizontal (Fig. 12). At this time the frame bore no carved decoration save for an incised lozenge pattern which is sometimes found.

Cane chairs were not expensive, and in London within very few years there was a strong demand for them, usually in sets comprising perhaps two armchairs with six or more single chairs. Construction was in the solid. Polished French walnut was used for the frames of the finer chairs; while beech, painted or japanned, or stained to resemble walnut, served as a (cheaper) substitute wood. (The manufacture of cane chairs, even at a late stage of their development, when they were no longer fashionable, would seem largely to have been confined to London. Defoe, in a well known passage, describing the furniture of a country tradesman stated: "... The Chairs, if of cane, are made in London; the ordinary matted chairs, perhaps in the place where they live.")[2]

The stylistic development of cane chairs is complex, and was very rapid. By about 1670 the height of the back was increased, and a broad flat top rail, or cresting, which was carved in low relief, was tenoned between the uprights. Then a deepened front stretcher rail was carved to correspond with the cresting, and the

---

[1] Quoted in full in *English Cane Chairs – Part 1*, by R. W. Symonds, in *The Connoisseur*, March 1951.
[2] *The Complete English Tradesman* (1745), by Daniel Defoe; edit. of 1841, Vol. I, p. 266.

framing of the back panel was similarly enriched, usually with a decoration of scrolls, flowers and foliage. The device of cupids supporting the crown was particularly popular and the description "carved with Boyes and Crowne" figures repeatedly in contemporary accounts. The motif, although associated with the Restoration of the monarchy was, in fact, in fashion until as late as about 1700. Arms were swept, and finished in deep scrolls, and an exuberant S-scroll form was incorporated in the design of front legs. By the end of the reign of Charles II, the carving was frequently pierced and executed in comparatively deep relief, with great gain in effect. Baluster turning was re-introduced as a popular alternative to twist turning. The mesh of the caning was finer, and some chairs were dished for flat squab cushions. Some of these features are exemplified in a cane seat in the form of two chairs in a private collection (Pl. 18c). This piece, nevertheless, was perhaps made about 1700: the design of the undulating crestings, and matching front rails, in particular, and of the baluster turned uprights, suggest a comparatively late date of origin. Seats of this description, which persumably were often supplied as part of a large set of seating furniture, are now extremely rare. This is an unusual and pleasing example. Designs were influenced by foreign fashions. It is significant that a number of chairs supplied to the Royal Palaces by Richard Price in the early 1680's were "turned of the Dutch turning". Generally, Dutch chairs may be distinguished from English by the character of the twist turning. The Dutch turning is thicker; the hollow is less pronounced. Moreover, two varieties of turning are sometimes found on the one chair. There is also in the great majority of cases a difference of construction: the stretcher which unites the back legs is placed high on English chairs – about midway between the seat rail and the ground; while in Dutch chairs it is either non-existent or is at the level of the side stretchers.

Under William and Mary the chair back was made even taller, and was narrower and surmounted by an elaborate cresting. The rake of the back was much increased; and the seat was smaller. The form of the cresting frequently matched that of the arched front stretcher rail; it was not, as formerly, secured between the uprights by means of mortice and tenon but rested on them and was attached by dowel-pegs. Dowel jointing was used also to secure the front legs, which were pegged to the base of the arm supports or, in the case of the single chair, to the underside of the seat rail. Structurally, these features are weak. The uprights were sometimes of baluster form, and occasionally fluted, and the arch of the cresting was repeated in the filling of the back which was caned in exceedingly fine mesh. Alternatively, the back was open-carved with a design of foliage and interlaced scrolls. The seats of many chairs of this latter type were upholstered. Covering materials included fine damasks and Genoese velvets. By the end of the century straight taper legs were introduced as a fashionable alternative to those of scroll form. These were of square moulded or round section, and finished in octagonal, spherical, or "Braganza" scrolled feet. Pear or mushroom-shaped cappings were a distinctive feature of the taper leg. The carved front rail was replaced by moulded diagonal stretchers of serpentine form meeting in a centre piece which was usually surmounted by a turned finial (Pl. 18B). The stretchers, ornamental in character and associated with chairs of fine quality, gave little additional strength to the legs. Tall upholstered single chairs of this ornate character were sometimes gilded.

Soon after 1700 the fashion for cane furniture declined. The industry nevertheless was securely established in London, and "Cane-Chair Shops", particularly those in St Paul's Churchyard and the near neighbourhood, continued to thrive. Cane chairs, stools, couches and tables, were supplied in quantity to innumerable households in England and were also exported to the Continent and to the American Colonies. Many pieces were based on models fashionable under William and Mary. They were simplified versions of these models, incorporating some new features. Cane chairs still figure in the Royal accounts under George I, although certainly they were not required for the private apartments. The cane furniture trade flourished until about 1740. In great part the continued wide popularity of cane furniture is to be explained by its cheapness. Chairs of beech were sold at a few shillings apiece. The claims of the chairmakers too had had much to recommend them: as stated, cane chairs were light and clean, and quite durable. But cane furniture was not readily to be obtained in all parts of the country. Communications were bad and many districts were almost completely isolated for long periods at a time. As a consequence country chairmakers had a market for chairs, of cane-chair pattern, which were upholstered in leather or cloth – as well as for rush-seated chairs with slatted backs. The former are interesting on two counts: firstly, by the not unattractive blending of new and old features of style and construction (such chairs are nearly always later in date than would appear at a glance) and secondly by evidence that they may provide as to the time-lag in fashion in the provinces. The plainly made chair illustrated in Fig. 13, now at Dennington Church, Suffolk, is reminiscent in general appearance of a type fashionable in the late seventeenth century. The tall back and shaped cresting, and the turned front stretcher rail, have the form and grace peculiar to the cane chair of that period, without its richness of ornamentation. The front legs are pegged to the bottom of the seat. The uprights to the back, however, are moulded and not turned, and the back panel and the seat upholstered simply with leather. The front supports, which are of hybrid cabriole form, and roughly shaped, are unusual; they point to a date of construction probably as late as the second quarter of the eighteenth century.

Chests of drawers. Veneered chests of drawers dating from the last quarter of the century are to be found in a variety of decorative woods – in figure walnut, kingwood, yew, burr elm and in a parquetry of oyster shells of walnut or laburnum, with a geometrical inlay of holly or boxwood.[1] Sycamore was often used as a

[1] See Edwards, *op. cit.*, Vol. II, p. 33 – *Chests of Drawers*, Fig. 29.

banding wood. Marquetry chests of drawers first appeared about 1680, and japanned examples a few years later.

The chest consisted usually of three long drawers, graduated in depth, with two short, shallow drawers above, and was supported on shaped bracket feet, or alternatively on ball or bun feet. The projecting ovolo moulding at the top of the chest was frequently repeated, inverted, at its base, immediately below the bottom drawer. Many chests were mounted on low stands, with four, five or six legs, tied

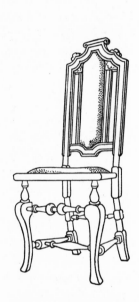

Fig. 13. Chair at Dennington Church, Suffolk. Early eighteenth century

Fig. 14. Walnut chest of drawers, on stand containing one long drawer, supported on plain cabriole legs, the drawer fronts veneered with figured walnut and bordered by herring-bone bandings. Early eighteenth century.

by stretchers. The stands, also, frequently contained drawers. Chests on stands rarely exceeded 5 ft. in height. The mouldings surrounding the drawer fronts, marking the divisions between drawers, were at this date applied *to the carcase*. A half-round moulding was commonly used on pieces dating from the end of the century; and was succeeded shortly after 1700 by a double half-round moulding. Mouldings were cross-banded. The carcase of the piece was usually of yellow deal, and drawer linings of oak or deal according to its quality. Normally, the grain of the wood of the bottom boards of the drawers ran from back to front and not from side to side of the piece. In many chests the sides were unveneered. The double chest or tallboy would seem not to have been made in England much before abou 1710.

The oak chest of four long drawers illustrated in Pl. 12C, although dating from the post-Restoration period, is joiner's work, and has therefore little in common with these fashionable specimens. Stylistic features of mixed date are interestingly combined in this piece. The legs of the low stand, while spirally turned, are tied by plain moulded stretchers of a type which had long been in general use. The distinctive decoration of the front of the chest, with raised panels of geometrical design, mitred and in strong projection, is in the style of the mid century. The brass escutcheon plates, and drop handles, are of a form introduced in the late seventeenth century.

Beds. By the late Stuart period, fashionable beds were taller, and luxuriously upholstered. The value of the four-post bed then lay almost entirely in its often very costly "clothes and hangings" – curtains and fringed valances of rich materials, and tester head-cloth; silk or linen inner curtains; blankets, rugs, quilts and counterpane; and flock, feather or down mattresses. Its wooden framework, the bedstead itself, was almost completely hidden. The bedposts were slender and, like the shaped head-board and tester, were covered with material. The state bed from Wroxton Abbey, now at Aston Hall, Birmingham, upholstered in red and gold brocade, is a fine example of this type of bed, dating from the end of the century (Pl. 16A). Beds of this nature were the products not of the cabinet maker or joiner but of the upholsterer. Their value was extremely high.

Mirrors. After the Restoration, looking-glass plates of a most satisfactory size and quality were being made at the Duke of Buckingham's Glass House at Vauxhall; they were sold at prices which were very much lower than those which formerly had obtained in England. Pepys for example bought with some satisfaction in December 1664 "a very fair glasse" for five guineas at the Old Exchange.

The mirror frame at this time was of square or rectangular proportions, and was surmounted by a semi-circular hood, sometimes pierced (which in many cases has not survived, having become detached from the body of the piece). The frame was broad, and of pronounced convex section. It was made by the cabinet-maker, or joiner, and was constructed of deal, veneered with cross-banded walnut, an oyster-shell parquetry of walnut, laburnum or olive wood. Various marquetry and japanned specimens still exist; these, being very decorative, must have been popular. Materials such as tortoiseshell and the imported incised lacquer were also occasionally employed for this type of frame (Pl. 17A).

Pier glasses. The pier glass, which was designed to be hung between windows above a side table of matching workmanship, was introduced towards the close of the century. It was sometimes 7 or 8 ft. high, and consequently of very tall proportions. Mirror and accompanying table were regarded as an interior architectural feature of the room. The pier-glass frame was flat, moulded and comparatively narrow, and was often decorated in gilt gesso. Sometimes the moulded frame was itself of glass.

Dressing mirrors. The dressing mirror on box stand (Pl. 17B) was a most serviceable introduction of the late seventeenth century; specimens of this small piece in veneered walnut, or japanned, were in general use within a few years.

A Queen Anne interior. *The Tea-Table*, a print which was first published at London in or about 1710,[1] provides some evidence as to the appearance of a contemporary interior. Therein we see "Thick Scandal circulate with right Bohea".[2] The room is richly but sparsely furnished. There is a foot carpet, which was an article of some scarcity at the beginning of the century, and an open alcove cupboard which apparently contains small pieces of china – "a neat booffett furnish'd" perhaps "with glasses and china for the table"[3] or with collectors' specimens of Chinese porcelain or Delft ware. The ladies in the room are seated in highbacked cane chairs at a gate-leg table of conventional design. Significantly, the chairs are of a type more often associated with the period of William and Mary than that of Anne. By contrast, the gesso wall mirror which hangs to the right of the fireplace is in the newest style.

3. THE QUEEN ANNE STYLE

Furniture which was in fashion under Queen Anne is characterized by a new restraint of form and ornament, and by a seeming simplicity. Enrichment of surface was gained by the use of figured veneers of walnut, and other woods, rather than by carved ornament or marquetry decoration. The flamboyant taste of the immediately preceding period – an expression of the first phase of English Baroque – underwent a sudden and considerable change about 1700, due in large part to the introduction of the cabriole support and to improving standards of craftsmanship. The cabriole rapidly superseded the scroll and the "Marot type" leg and was applied to chairs (Pl. 18A and Fig. 11) and settees, tables, tripods, stands and other articles of furniture, with decisive effect on design and construction. On fine pieces, stretchers were often dispensed with, not to be re-introduced until the beginning of the second half of the eighteenth century. In no other article of furniture perhaps, is design so finely and nicely adjusted as in the developed "hoop-back"

---

[1] *The Tea-Table*, a print measuring $6\frac{1}{4} \times 5\frac{3}{8}$ in., published *c.* 1710 and sold by John Bowles of 13, Cornhill, London. See *Catalogue of Prints and Drawings in the British Museum. Division I: Political and Personal Satires*, Vol. II, 1873, No. 1555.

[2] Tea had been introduced into the country from Holland about the time of the Restoration, and was at this date drunk in private houses only by the well-to-do. It was still very expensive, and the Bohea was priced at more than 30s. per lb.

[3] *The Journeys of Celia Fiennes*, ed. by Christopher Morris, 1947, p. 345. A house at Epsom (London and the Later Journeys, *c.* 1701–3).

single chair, the well-defined serpentine curves of which, by nature ornamental, are governed by structural purpose – the vase or fiddle-shaped splat, enclosed by undulating uprights and shaped to the form of the user's back, and the seat rail, often rounded in front, supported on graceful cabriole legs finishing in club feet.

An appreciable increase in domestic comfort in this reign was due in part to the introduction of new and useful pieces, and to the development of those but newly adopted.

Small walnut bureaux on open stands with turned legs were made first towards 1700. (Extant specimens, which are now exceedingly scarce, are usually of very fine quality and workmanship.)[1] Bureaux on chests (pieces constructed with a base of two or three long and two short drawers, or with a base containing a central kneehole) were in general production in the early eighteenth century, particularly in a "stock size" of 3 ft. 6 in., and have survived in comparatively large numbers, together with tall bureaux in two stages, or bureaux bookcases, which in form are closely related to them. The cupboard doors of the upper stage of these latter pieces were faced often with mirror glass, and the surmounting cornices were alternatively straight, hooded or pedimented. The bureau bookcase illustrated in Pl. 16B is a fine specimen and of striking appearance. It is veneered with the burr wood of mulberry, decorated with cross bandings bordered by inlaid pewter stringing lines. The technique is distinctive and the bureau bookcase may be attributed to John Coxed, or to Coxed and Woster, working at the White Swan in St Paul's Churchyard, London, in the early eighteenth century, on the basis of its close similarity in form and materials to other known (labelled) pieces made by this firm.[2]

This cabinet is significant of the rapid development of the cabinet-maker's craft which had come about within a generation, and evidence of technical skill.[3] The reticent character of much early eighteenth-century case furniture is to be seen in the walnut chest on stand which is illustrated in Fig. 14. The chest is distinguished by fine proportions, and by its quality of workmanship; and the matched, figured veneers of the front provide the main enrichment. By the early eighteenth century foreign styles had become assimilated and naturalized. The best walnut furniture of the Queen Anne period is direct and unaffected in character. The sets of chairs and upholstered settees with open arms, side-and dressing-tables, card-tables and bureaux, made for the upper and middle classes have consistently a purity of style hitherto unrealized in England.

---

[1] See *English Furniture Styles*, by Ralph Fastnedge, Pelican Books, 1955, Pl. 23.

[2] John Coxed was succeeded by G. Coxed and T. Woster (*fl. c.* 1710–36). After Woster's death in 1736, these famous premises were occupied by Henry Bell. See *Georgian Cabinet-Makers*, by R. Edwards and M. Jourdain, 1954, for fuller details.

[3] Smaller cabinets, with fall-fronts, which were inspired by foreign models and were known as "scriptors" or "scrutoirs", enjoyed great popularity during both the late Stuart and Anne periods. These cabinets, which are found often veneered in burr walnut or decorated with floral marquetry, were supported either on a base of drawers or on an open stand, and rarely exceeded 5 ft. 9 in. in height. Some cabinets were constructed with a pair of hinged doors in place of the fall-front.

EARLY GEORGIAN

IN order to appreciate fully the general character of English furniture-making in the period 1714–60, it is necessary to examine it against the social and economic background of the time. This was the period of the ascendancy of the Whigs, whose careful commercial and financial policy led to increased prosperity, especially for merchants and the landowning classes. Wealthy people were often anxious to spend lavishly on new houses and furniture which would embellish or raise their social status, and to meet this demand the furniture industry expanded considerably. The centre of the industry was, of course, London, which, as well as being the capital and the principal port, was of more importance and influence in relation to the rest of the country than it has been since. This is explained by its great size; in the middle of the century, while Bristol and Norwich, the next two largest cities, had some 50,000 inhabitants each, London had well over half a million. Here were found the largest single area for the production of furniture, and the main source of new ideas and styles. To London were attracted craftsmen of ability and ambition from the provinces, and from London the best furniture which was then being made in this country was sent to wealthy people throughout the kingdom, both by land and sea. A considerable export trade in every kind of furniture to world-wide markets was also developing during this period.

But, apart from the great capital city, England was still predominantly a country of villages and hamlets, of a society essentially rural in character; its towns were small by modern standards, though some were growing. The static and isolated nature of rural life is largely explained by the poor state of inland communications, for the great era of road improvements and canal-building did not begin until after 1760. In this kind of society most of the furniture used by all classes of the people, except the rich, was made locally. In the villages the furniture of cottages and farm-houses was made by the householder himself, or by the village joiner, who worked on traditional lines and paid little, if any, heed to the changing fashions of the towns. In the provincial towns the best cabinet-makers, some of whom were very capable craftsmen, supplied the lesser gentry and middle classes with good, well-made furniture which reflected something of the latest fashions from London; the less-skilled cabinet-makers, catering for ordinary townspeople,

49

D

made unpretentious furniture which might be humbler adaptations of pieces that
had been fashionable years – often many years – previously.

Furniture-making in London. In London there was a tremendous diversity in
the nature of the shops, in the types of goods which they sold and in the skill of the
craftsmen who made the furniture. It is clear that there were significant changes in
shopkeeping. Some shops were notably growing in size, and required considerable
capital to stock them. The furniture of the highest quality came from the shops
where an eminent craftsman (or two craftsmen, for partnerships were common)
controlled the business; but other large shops were directed by a shopkeeper who
was not a craftsman at all, and did not even employ craftsmen on his premises to
make the furniture, but obtained his goods for re-sale from outside craftsmen.
Dealers of this kind had existed for a long time in the furniture trades, but during
this period the scope of their business was widening appreciably. An anonymous
writer in 1747, discussing London trades, described cabinet-makers as follows:
"Many of their shops are so richly set out that they look more like Palaces and
their Stocks are of exceeding great Value. But this Business seems to consist, as do
many others, of two Branches, the Maker and the Vendor; for the Shopkeeper does
not always make every sort of Goods that he deals in, though he bears away the
Title." The same writer noted that turners could be divided into two classes: the
"Real Mechanics" who were the craftsmen, and a "Set of Shopkeepers, many of
them in a very large way [who] engross, as to the buying and selling part, all the
produce of the real Turners and many Trades besides."[1]

The more fashionable craftsmen tended to work in the same area. In the earlier
part of the century the chief centre was St Paul's Churchyard, but by about 1750
many of the leading craftsmen, among them Goodison, Hallett, Chippendale, Vile
and Cobb, were working in St Martin's Lane and Long Acre. Some of their
premises were very imposing. "The corner house of Longacre", wrote J. T. Smith
in 1828, "formed a small part of the extensive premises formerly occupied by that
singularly haughty character, Cobb, the Upholsterer."[2] The secret of the fine
furniture which came from these shops lay in the great skill of the craftsmen who
worked in them, each man specializing in a particular branch of his craft. This
division of labour was carried on to a greater degree in London than elsewhere.
The workman in furniture who had no specialist training was regarded as of very
inferior status – "no more than a cobbling Carpenter or Joiner". To illustrate this
specialization, the comments of the writer of 1747, already quoted, on the sub-
divisions of one single craft, that of chair-making, are worth noting: "Though this
Sort of Household Goods is generally sold at the Shops of Cabinet-makers for all
the better kinds, and at the Turners for the more common, yet there are particular
Makers for each. The Cane-chair-makers not only make this Sort (now almost out

---

[1] *General Description of All Trades*, Anon., 1747.
[2] *Nollekins and his Times*, by J. T. Smith, 1828.

of Use) but the better Sort of matted, Leather-bottomed and Wooden Chairs, of which there is great Variety in Goodness, Workmanship and Price; and some of the Makers, who are also Shopkeepers, are very considerable Dealers, employing from £300 to upwards of £500 in Trade. The white Wooden, Wickers and ordinary matted Sort, commonly called Kitchen-chairs, and sold by the Turners, are made by different Hands, but are all inferior Employs. Those covered with Stuff, Silks, etc., are made and sold by the Upholsterers." Other kinds of craftsmen employed in chair-making could be added to this list, such as chair-carvers, gilders and japanners.

Overseas trade. London was the main centre of the export trade in all kinds of furniture and upholstery which were sent throughout Europe and to the colonies. Most of the emigrants who left this country to settle permanently in the colonies took some household furniture with them. Richer people, such as merchants, planters and colonial governors, took a great deal of furniture of the best quality. An interesting example of this practice is shown in Pl. 23, a view of the Supper Room in the Governor's Palace, Williamsburg, Virginia, as it was in the mid-eighteenth century. The furniture, brought from England by successive governors, is mainly of the Queen Anne and Chippendale periods.[1] These wealthier people frequently had other supplies of furniture sent out to them from home. Cabinet-makers in the American colonies also imported fashionable furniture from England to sell with their own products.

London was the chief importing centre for a whole range of goods which were required by the furniture industry. These included the many kinds of timbers and raw materials of the upholsterers – brocades, velvets, feathers for beds, etc. – as well as foreign articles (carpets, pictures, etc.) which were sold in some of the shops.

Kent and the Baroque. In the second quarter of the century the great figure in furniture design was William Kent (1685–1748), the first English architect who included furniture as an integral part of his interior decoration. His versatility as a designer was thus described by Horace Walpole: "He was not only consulted for furniture, as frames for pictures, glasses, tables, chairs, but for plate, for a barge, for a cradle."[2] He was the leading exponent of the Palladian revival which was sponsored by his patron, the Earl of Burlington, the "Apollo of the Arts". In the great Palladian house of the period, of which Raynham, Holkham and Houghton are celebrated examples, as well as in those parts of the royal palaces which he helped to furnish, Kent made free use of the rich and ornate baroque style which he had studied during his travels in Italy. He emphasized the bold and massive

---

[1] *Williamsburg: a Restored Colonial Capital*, by H. Comstock, Connoisseur Year Book, 1954.
[2] *Anecdotes of Painting*, by H. Walpole, 1762–71.

treatment of furniture, employing large, elaborately carved festoons, mouldings and masks, in soft woods richly gilt, or in mahogany parcel-gilt. Monumental side-tables, with large marble tops imported from Italy were his speciality. His furniture may be criticized as extravagant and florid – "immeasurably ponderous", according to Walpole – yet it is perfectly in place with the particular settings for which it was designed, and in relation to which it should always be judged (Pl. 19). It was made for a small privileged group of wealthy clients, but the influence of its style is noticeable in the general architectural character of much of the best furniture made by leading cabinet-makers after 1725. In 1740 Kent's style was adapted to furniture of the middle classes by the Langley brothers in their trade publication (see **design books** below).

The Kent period was the great age of English gilding, and much furniture was gesso-gilt. Gesso was a mixture of whiting and parchment size which was applied in layers on a basis of soft woods. When the composition was hard, a pattern was formed in relief by working away the ground; the whole surface was then gilded or, more rarely, silvered (Pls. 20A, 24).

The mid-century styles. The reaction against the Baroque set in towards the middle of the century and took the form of a medley of styles: the Rococo, Chinese and Gothic. It is important to remember that these styles had quite different histories and that it is inaccurate to consider the Rococo as the parent of the other two. But in many respects there were affinities between them which do much to explain their vogue. They stressed the lighter treatment to fanciful, capricious ornament in which their respective contributions could be blended. At this point some of the observations of Hogarth in his *Analysis of Beauty* (published in 1753) are interesting. He exalted waving and serpentine forms. "The waving line", he wrote, "...is a line more productive of beauty than any of the former (i.e. straight and circular lines) ... for which reason we shall call it the line of beauty. The serpentine line hath the power of super-adding grace to beauty." Together their beauty and grace produced intricacy in form – "that peculiarity in the lines which compose it, that leads the eye a wanton kind of chace". He also wrote of "infinite variety" as an apt summary of beauty. Though he expressed approval of the Gothic ("have not many gothic buildings a great deal of consistent beauty in them?"), he decried both the Palladian and Chinese styles. He was also a bigoted anglophil in his prejudices against French influences, and it must be admitted, as Walpole wrote, that his views "did not carry the conviction nor meet the universal acquiescence he expected". But, all things considered, his ideas might be said to amount to a tacit approval of the rococo taste, and they certainly reflected something of the prevailing mood.

Rococo. Rococo decoration in English furniture sprang from the French *rocaille*, among the outstanding creators of which were Pierre Lepautre with his transformation of baroque material about 1700, and J. A. Meissonier and Nicholas Pineau, who gave the movement a new phase about 1730. Lepautre employed delicate linear ornament in slight relief. To this Pineau's *genre pittoresque* added asymmetrical decoration in intricate curves and C scrolls. Thus the new style was in marked contrast to the baroque accentuation of plastic forms. In France the principal sphere of this movement in its early stages had been interior decoration, "in England, where classicism was so strongly entrenched, the fire of the French Rococo made but small inroads, chiefly in furniture".[1] It appeared in its most characteristic form in this country on sconces, mirrors, picture-frames and console tables, all elaborately carved and gilded by specialist craftsmen (Pl. 21). These pieces were closely related to French models, but in case furniture (unless French furniture was being deliberately copied) a more independent approach was evident; the ornament became less exuberant and usually took the form of delicate carving. The credit for introducing the style to furniture here belongs to Matthias Lock, in whose pattern-books, published from 1740 onwards, rococo decoration was applied to various small pieces of furniture of a limited range. The new mode was catching on in the late 'forties, and in 1754 it became the predominant style with the publication of Chippendale's *Director*, in which the "modern taste" was applied to domestic furniture of all kinds. It was still the prevailing form in the third edition of the *Director* in 1762, but by then it was giving way to Robert Adam's neo-classical style.

Chinoiserie. In the 'forties there was a revival of the enthusiasm for *chinoiseries* which had been prevalent in the later seventeenth century. The extent of the revival was thus described, with some exaggeration, by a writer in *The World* in 1753: "According to the present prevailing whim every thing is Chinese, or in the Chinese taste; or, as it is sometimes more modestly expressed, 'partly after the Chinese manner'. Chairs, tables, chimney-pieces, frames for looking-glasses, and even our most vulgar utensils are all reduced to this new-fangled standard." He went on to note how freely Chinese designs had been adapted by English craftsmen: "Our Chinese ornaments are not only of our own manufacture but, what has seldom been attributed to the English, of our own invention." This interest in oriental fashions had been renewed to some extent by travel books, the chief of which was du Halde's description of the Empire of China, translated from the French in 1741. On furniture, *chinoiseries* took many forms: mirrors had pagodas, long-necked birds, icicles and small oriental figures; chairs had pagoda crestings and lattice-work backs; and other pieces – tables, cabinets, bookcases, etc. – had frets, open or applied, in a continuous geometric pattern (Pl. 26A). Japanned furniture, which had not previously gone out of fashion so much as other *chinoiseries*, was now very popular (Pl. 28A). The more bizarre aspects of the vogue were much criticized by contemporaries, as the above passage shows. In 1756 Angeloni

[1] *The Creation of the Rococo*, by F. Kimball, 1943.

(in reality J. Shebbeare writing as an Italian) complained that "the simple and sublime have lost all influence almost every where, all is Chinese or gothic; every chair in an apartment, the frames of glasses, and tables, must be Chinese: the walls covered with Chinese paper fill'd with figures which resemble nothing in God's creation, and which a prudent nation would prohibit for the sake of pregnant women".[1] The craze was on the decline by 1765, but while it lasted it had a great deal in common with the Rococo and was often skilfully blended with it.

Gothic. The "Gothic Revival" of the mid-century will always be connected with Horace Walpole and Strawberry Hill, which he began to turn into a gothic villa in 1750, and of which the first stage in the transformation was complete in 1753. But it must be stressed that Walpole was not entirely a pioneer, for interest in the gothic style had long pre-dated Strawberry Hill. There was still a living tradition of gothic building and decoration which had persisted since medieval times, in spite of the Reformation and the classical Renaissance. This, however, had little influence on Walpole's ideas. Preceding Walpole, too, was a strong "gothic" trend in literature, while the gothic work of architects of the classical school, as late as Hawksmoor and Kent, had further stimulated interest in medieval forms. What Walpole did was to make a particular contribution to the movement. He was the first patron of the Gothic who copied original medieval work for interior decoration, and his social position ensured that his new fashions would be widely imitated among the upper classes. He adapted gothic motifs in accordance with prevailing taste and turned them into a "Rococo Gothic" which he himself described as "more the works of fancy than imitation". In the *Director* this gothic mode appeared in various forms on furniture, usually as carved crocketed pinnacles, carved and fretwork arches and arcading, and arched glazing bars. The style was considered by *The World* in 1753 as unfashionable ("a few years ago everything was gothic"), but this judgement was altogether too premature, for gothic pieces and decoration were illustrated in the third edition of the *Director* in 1762, and indeed the gothic taste (like *chinoiseries*) found some favour during the rest of the Georgian period.

The design books. The fourth and fifth decades of the century saw the publication of many books of engraved furniture designs. At first these designs were incorporated in pattern books produced by architects, builders and artists, and not by craftsmen, and the relatively few furniture plates which were shown were part of general decorative schemes and were of very varied merit. One of the earliest books of this kind was Batty and Thomas Langley's *City and Country Builder's and Workman's Treasury of Designs*, published in 1740 (with plates dated 1739). It was mainly concerned with architecture, but included designs for side-tables with marble tops, table-frames, a chest of drawers, a medal case, a dressing-table and

---

[1] *Letters on the English Nation*, by B. Angeloni (J. Shebbeare), 1756.

several bookcases. In most of these pieces the baroque style of the Kent school was clearly evident; there were, however, a few designs of French tables (one of them after Pineau) with rococo influences. As has been pointed out, the pioneer of the Rococo in England was Matthias Lock, who produced several design books between 1740 and 1752. In this latter year, in which he published *A New Book of Ornaments* in collaboration with Henry Copland, the Rococo has been applied to carvers' pieces, notably mirrors, pier-tables, clock-cases, stands and wall-lights. The Chinese taste was catered for by several pattern books which appeared in the 'fifties, particularly by Matthias Darly, and by William Halfpenny and his son John. The Halfpennys published some plates with Chinese chair designs in their *Rural Architecture in the Chinese Taste* in 1750–55, and Darly had a few illustrations of furniture in his *New Book of Chinese Designs* in 1754. An attempt – not a very successful one – to apply to seat furniture the various styles of the time was made by Darly in 1750–51, in the *New Book of Chinese, Gothic and Modern Chairs*.

Chippendale's "Director". A landmark was reached in English furniture history with the publication of Thomas Chippendale's *The Gentleman and Cabinet-Maker's Director* in 1754, for it was the first pattern book to be devoted entirely to furniture, and the first to be published by a cabinet-maker. A second edition (virtually a reprint) appeared in 1755, and a third in 1762; and it was followed by a number of similar publications. It has made Chippendale's name a household word, and practically synonymous with the rococo style of the mid-century. But although Chippendale's signature appeared on the plates, it seems that he cannot claim sole credit for all the designs, for it is now known that he employed Lock and Copland as his "ghosts" to help him.[1] He must, however, be given his fair share of praise both for his keen business sense in turning to good account the growing popularity of the rococo style, and for applying it to all kinds of furniture, including articles for ordinary domestic use. As a practical craftsman his knowledge and experience must have been of the greatest value to the draughtsmen in his employ, and he adapted the French mode into an unmistakable English version, and did not merely imitate it. In the *Director* the Chinese and gothic styles were exploited to a secondary degree; the title-page of the third edition omitted reference to these styles, though some of their plates were retained. It is through the success of his book that the reputation of Chippendale has overshadowed those of his rivals. His firm was certainly a celebrated one, with a rich and influential clientele, but, so far as is known, he did not supply any furniture to the royal household, and it is noteworthy that the best work of his firm was done, not in the *Director* styles, but in the neo-classic style which superseded the rococo in the 'sixties.

Leading cabinet-makers. Recent research has brought into prominence those

[1] *The Creators of the Chippendale Style*, by F. Kimball and E. Donnell, Metropolitan Museum Studies, 1929.

cabinet-makers of the early Georgian period whose workshops produced the best-quality furniture. Among the most important in George I's reign were the two partners, John Gumley and James Moore, Gumley specializing in mirrors and Moore in gesso work. In 1715 Steele (in *The Lover*) wrote of Gumley's show-rooms over the New Exchange in the Strand that "it is not in the Power of any Potentate in Europe to have so beautiful a Mirror as he may purchase here for a trifle". It is proof of Gumley's business acumen that he left a large fortune. In George II's reign a prominent cabinet-maker was Benjamin Goodison of Long Acre, who made furniture for the Royal Family for a long period, from 1727 to 1767; but the most fashionable cabinet-maker of the reign seems to have been William Hallett of St Martin's Lane and Long Acre. Walpole's wellknown reference to Hallett's "mongrel Chinese" indicates that he worked in that style and also that his name was widely known. Special mention should be made of the partnership of William Vile and John Cobb, who were the foremost craftsmen in the period 1755–65. From their premises in St Martin's Lane, close to Chippendale's, came some of the very finest furniture of the whole Georgian era. There seems to have been some degree of specialization within the firm, Vile (who was senior partner) being responsible for carved work (in which he is the acknowledged master, for his work in the Rococo surpassed that of Chippendale). Reference to some outstanding masterpieces of this firm is made below. A craftsman of a different kind was Giles Grendey of Clerkenwell, who made good furniture during George II's reign, including japanned pieces for export.

Woods: the introduction of mahogany. A significant event occurred in 1721, when the Government passed an Act (8 Geo. I, c. 12) which abolished the heavy import duties on practically all the timbers from British colonies in North America and the West Indies. The purpose of the Act was to increase the supplies of timber for shipbuilding, but cabinet-makers naturally took advantage of the lower prices, and one of the chief results was to stimulate the trade in mahogany. This wood had been known in England for over a century, but only a very little had been used for furniture. The importance of the Act can be measured by the rise of the value of mahogany shipped to England, from £43 in 1720 to £277 in 1722, £1,237 in 1724, £6,430 in 1735 and to almost £30,000 in 1750. As the supplies of mahogany increased and its many fine properties advertised themselves, it gradually – but only gradually – supplanted walnut as the most fashionable wood for furniture. It had a beautiful patina which improved with the rub of use; a metallic strength which considerably affected furniture design towards the middle of the century (chair-backs in the rococo and Chinese styles provide excellent examples of this); an attractive range of colours and figures; a strong resistance to decay; and a great width of board which made it ideal for table-tops, cabinet doors and similar pieces. It was being used by the royal cabinet-makers in 1724, and in 1743 Mark Catesby wrote that the "Excellency of this Wood for all Domestick Uses is now

sufficiently known in England".[1] There were many sources of supply in the West
Indies and Central America, including the Spanish colonies, whence the timber
was smuggled here via the British settlements to avoid the duty on foreign wood.
At first San Domingo mahogany was chiefly used – a hard, dense wood with little
figure. About 1750 it was generally superseded by the Cuban variety, which was
easier to work, and had a dark, rich colour and fine figures; this meant more use
of veneers instead of solid work, common with San Domingo wood. Honduras
mahogany, lighter in weight and colour, was mainly used in the second half of the
century.

It has been frequently stated that cabinet-makers turned to mahogany because
walnut was in short supply. This is inaccurate, for there was no lack of supplies of
good European walnut for veneers or of American ("black" or "Virginia") walnut
for work in the solid. Much furniture veneered with European walnut was made
throughout the first half of the century, but considerable amounts have perished
through worm, and it is this fact which has led to the supposition that walnut was
replaced by mahogany earlier than in fact it was. Between 1725 and 1750 walnut
and mahogany were perhaps equally fashionable in London (Pl. 28B).

Other woods. In 1747 Campbell quoted the typical London timber merchant
as "furnished with Deal from Norway; with Oak and Wainscot from Sweden; and
some from the Counties of England; with Mahogany from Jamaica; with Wallnut-
Tree from Spain".[2] This was a fair sample of the timber stocks which might be found
in a fashionable cabinet-maker's yard, but the list of their places of origin could
be enlarged. Yellow deal from the Baltic was used as carcase work for veneers, but
after about 1750 red deal from North America came into more general use for this
purpose. Good imported oak was used for drawer linings. Among other imported
woods mention can be made of rosewood, sometimes used for solid work, and
padouk, which was occasionally used after 1725. For gilding and japanning, car-
cases of deal, beech, lime and sometimes pear were employed, while chair-frames
for this purpose were usually of beech. Beech was also common for the cheaper
kinds of chairs.

The country craftsmen worked with native woods, such as oak, elm, ash, birch,
beech and fruit woods. For Windsor chairs the woods commonly found were yew
for frames, beech or ash for spindles, and elm for seats.

Fashionable furniture: chairs. The chairs designed by Kent for his wealthy
clients were usually of walnut or mahogany parcel gilt, or of soft woods entirely gilt
and had a great deal of mask, foliage and shell ornament (Pl. 19). But apart from
these the design of chairs in the early Georgian period followed the Queen Anne
tradition and was very little affected at first by the coming of mahogany. The
cabriole leg with either the club foot or, on finer specimens, the ball-and-claw or

---

[1] *The Natural History of Carolina, Florida and the Bahama Islands*, by M. Catesby, 1731–43.
[2] *The London Tradesman*, by R. Campbell, 1747.

lion's paw, continued to be fashionable throughout the first half of the century. After about 1725 carving became more elaborate and often took the form of the lion-and-satyr mask, or shell and pendant on the knee-piece and centre of the seat, and of the eagle's head at the end of the arms. Chair-backs, however, began to show more distinct changes from the earlier examples; the solid splat was replaced by an open design which at first was in the form of vertical piercing, and the hoop shape of the top rail became flatter and almost square at the corners.

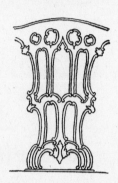

Fig. 16 (*above*). Gothic chair-back.

Fig. 15 (*right*). Chair leg with scroll foot and cabochon ornament on knee, fashionable *c.* 1750.

As mahogany became more widely used its great strength led to daring carving and piercing on chair-backs and considerable changes in design had taken place by 1750. Chairs in the rococo style had carved open-work splats with much delicate ornament, which were generally varieties of C and S scrolls under a top rail of serpentine ("cupid's bow") form. The cabriole leg was retained, but the scroll foot was now often employed (Fig. 15). Among the most celebrated examples in this style were the "ribband-backs" which were introduced in the *Director* and had interlaced ribbon designs intricately carved, sometimes joining the side uprights. On some chairs of this period the straight leg was used and stretchers were re-introduced (though they were unnecessary from the structural point of view) after a lapse of some fifty years.

Chinese chairs had large-scale latticework in the backs (Pl. 26A) and in the space between the arms and seats, and they often had a pagoda shaping for the top rails. Their legs were generally square in shape with frets, either in low-relief carving in the solid, or pierced. Another of their distinctive features was the use of brackets, fret-cut, in the angles between the legs and seats. Gothic chairs had interlaced pointed arches in the centre splat or in the whole space between the uprights (Fig. 16).

Upholstered chairs of the early Georgian period normally had plain over stuffed backs and seats, and some arms were padded on the horizontal member (Pl. 26D). The *Director* shows several examples of "French" upholstered armchairs with stuffed backs, arms of various shapes, and light, graceful versions of the cabriole leg. Carved motifs, among which the acanthus leaf was prominent, are found on the knees, seat rails, arms and cresting rails (Pl. 26c).

Chests of drawers, commodes, tallboys. Two main types of chests of drawers can be distinguished in this period – the plain, rectangular kind of traditional design, and the more elaborate variety influenced by the French commode. During the first half of the century there was little change in the former class; walnut continued to be the chief wood employed in making them, with some mahogany after 1730, and the usual construction was of four or five drawers of full width, and bracket, or, more occasionally, cabriole-form feet. Mouldings were now to be found on the edges of drawers, and not on the rails between drawers. At first drawer edges had the lip moulding which had come into fashion about 1710, but after 1730 it was gradually replaced by the cock-bead, which was almost exclusively used from about 1745 until the end of the century. After 1750 taller chests of drawers became fashionable, with five or six drawers, of which two, of half width, were at the top. When mahogany veneers were used, they were generally put on a carcase of deal, and drawer linings were of good-quality oak.

Commodes became popular when the full impact of French influence was felt. In fact, "commode" was the name applied about the middle of the century to all kinds of decorative furniture fitted with drawers, so much so that "chest of drawers" was rarely used in the trade catalogues of the period (it is mentioned only once – on Plate CXIII – in the third edition of the *Director*). For convenience, commodes can be taken here to refer to the fashionable drawing-room pieces showing unmistakable French character.

These early commodes were of mahogany enriched with carving on the frieze, feet, corners and drawer fronts. In the period 1740–50 some extremely fine examples have been attributed to William Vile. Pl. 25A illustrates a less elaborate specimen in the rococo style. It is serpentine fronted and has handles in the French taste; the carving appears on the canted corners, on the rail beneath the top drawers and on the plinth. In other pieces of this kind the edges of the top were often gadrooned. Some commodes were japanned, especially those intended for bedrooms in the Chinese taste in large houses. A fine example, formerly at Badminton House, is shown in Pl. 28A; besides the japanning, it has the pierced fret and lattice-work typical of this style.

Tallboys or chests-on-chests followed the same lines as the plainer chests of drawers. The large cavetto moulding on the cornice remained until about 1735, after which date the flat frieze came into fashion. This frieze was often decorated with applied frets, as were the canted corners (or the latter might be fluted). Feet, handles and drawer-edge mouldings were similar to those on the chests of drawers described above.

Tables. The large number of different kinds of tables in use at this time may conveniently be reduced to the following main categories: dining-, side-, tea-, card- and library.

Early in George II's reign, dining-tables, in walnut or mahogany, were still constructed on the gate-leg principle and had, in the larger examples, six cabriole legs, of which two – one on each side – could swing out to support the flaps. Usually the tops were oval or circular in shape. About the middle of the century another and more convenient version of the large table came into use. This was a composite piece of three units: a centre gate-leg table with rectangular flaps, and two semi-circular side-tables which could be fitted to the centre when required. There are no illustrations of dining-tables in the *Director*, presumably because they allowed little scope for showing the decorative features of the fashions then in vogue.

The term side-tables may be taken to refer to the ornamental tables which stood against the walls of the best rooms of the larger houses of the period, and they include console-tables, which were normally supported by two brackets but had no rear legs, and pier-tables, which occupied the pier or wall between two windows. In the earlier part of the century, preceding the baroque phase, but showing traces of the same kind of decoration, appeared some attractive gesso side-tables, one of which, dating from the period *c.* 1710–20, is shown in Pl. 24A. This is an excellent example of the kind of work done in gesso, but it is unusual in that it is silvered and not gilt. The top of this table has the monogram of the original owner carved in the centre.

The carved and gilt side-tables designed by Kent were perhaps the best example of his work in the baroque style, and were influenced by the pieces which he had seen in the palaces of Venetia. Monumental in size, they had scroll legs with acanthus, scale and guilloche decoration, or the supports might be female figures, animals, etc., joined by swags of leaves, fruit and flowers. For the tops, in addition to marble (whence the description "marble tables"), gesso, mosaic or scagliola were used. The latter was an artificial composition of plaster of Paris and glue into which small pieces of marble were worked; the whole could be coloured and highly polished. The friezes of these tables were carved with classical motifs, among which the Vitruvian scroll was prominent.

As the rococo style replaced the baroque the massive side-tables gradually went out of favour. After 1740 a more restrained treatment was generally evident, even though some early rococo examples carried a certain amount of lavish ornament. A mahogany side-table of *c.* 1745 is illustrated in Pl. 25B. It has a marble top, a mask in the centre of the frieze and female heads on the scrolled legs. Rococo-style side-tables in the *Director* keep the cabriole legs, while those in the Chinese and gothic tastes have straight legs. The Chinese varieties have fretwork on the frieze and legs (pierced in some cases on the latter). Marble remained in great demand for the tops of these tables.

Console-tables (or "clap"-tables, as they were then called) were introduced into this country from France early in the century. In the baroque phase some elaborate specimens were produced, with supports in the form of an eagle with out-

Fig. 17. Console table with marble top, Vitruvian scroll on frieze and eagle support decorated with gilt gesso, *c.* 1730.

stretched wings, or of a pair of intertwined dolphins (Fig. 17). There were also ornate examples in the later rococo taste, giving full rein to the prevailing asymmetrical decoration. None that was made, however, seems quite to have matched the highly intricate designs which are presented for these tables in the *Director*, where they go by the name of "Frames for Marble Slabs".

Card-playing for money was a popular pastime in high society in the early Georgian period, and in consequence many fine card-tables were produced by the cabinet-makers. From early in the century the most usual type was that with a folding top on cabriole legs. At the beginning of George I's reign the folding frame, with a concertina action, replaced the former method by which one leg was swung out to support the flap. The corners of the tables were at first rounded and were dished to hold candlesticks; they also had extra wells for money or counters. In some examples there were separate candle-brackets which swung out from the frieze. About 1730, when mahogany was coming into use for tables of this kind, square corners were introduced, and remained popular until about 1760. Early mahogany tables had lion heads carved on the knee-pieces, and occasionally the frieze was serpentine. Rococo decoration took the form of carved coquillage and acanthus leaves on the frieze and legs, gadrooning on the borders (Fig. 18) and a more graceful cabriole leg, often with a scroll foot. Pl. 28B shows an example of

Fig. 18. Gadrooning, a carved ornamental edging in vogue, c. 1750.

c. 1750 on which the ball-and-claw foot is retained. It also illustrates the square corners of the period, and is a late example of the use of walnut, for it has figured walnut veneers on an oak carcase. Other card-tables often had Chinese and gothic motifs, and in these cases, as with side-tables, the legs were straight.

The custom of tea-drinking had been spreading rapidly since the end of the seventeenth century. In George II's reign the many tea-gardens which had sprung up in and around London fell into disrepute among people of fashion, who consequently carried on the habit in their own homes – an example which was soon copied by other classes. Hence the development of small "china-tables", as tea-tables were then called, of which two main varieties can be distinguished: those with oblong tops, and those with round tops on a pillar and claw, i.e. tripod base. The oblong tops were frequently mounted on dainty cabriole legs with ball-and-claw feet, or on straight legs, often pierced, if in the Chinese taste (Fig. 19). Little galleries, which were in many cases fretted, ran round the edges of these tables. Tripod tables had either similar galleries, or scalloped and carved ("piecrust") edges. These raised edges were to prevent the fragile tea-things from being swept off. Pl. 22A illustrates a mahogany tripod table of c. 1745 with the characteristic turned and carved pillar and ball-and-claw feet. The small platform beneath the "piecrust" top is wedged to the upper part of the pillar; this wedge can be removed to enable the table-top to be lifted off. Two designs in the *Director* bear the description: "Tables for holding China, and may be used as Tea-Tables". These tables were oblong in shape with serpentine edges. One design has cross stretchers with rococo carving, and both have galleries which could be either plain or fretted.

Large pedestal library tables came into general use in the second quarter of the century for the libraries of the great Palladian houses. Tables of this type had already appeared in the late seventeenth century, and were modelled on the French pieces which had been made in the reign of Louis XIV, but they did not attempt either the intricate Buhl work or the ormolu work which distinguished the finest French examples. Instead, they were made of mahogany with lavishly carved mouldings and terminals which were sometimes gilded. The centres of the tables were left open, or occasionally contained a cupboard; the pedestals had drawers and cupboards; and particular care was taken over the decoration, as they were designed to stand in the middle of the library. The elaborate terminals were seldom found after about 1740, and a lighter kind of carving then became more usual. In

Fig. 19. Mahogany "china" or tea table with fretwork gallery, c. 1750.

the Chippendale period library tables were very much in demand, for the third edition of the *Director* shows eleven examples, all of the open pedestal type, compared with six in the first edition. Various forms of rococo, Chinese and gothic decoration are illustrated. Rococo influence is evident in the contemporary example in Pl. 29B.

Throughout the whole of this period the smaller knee-hole writing-table, with drawers on each side of the central recess, continued in favour. Two of this type are illustrated by Chippendale under the name of "commode-buroe" tables.

Bookcases. In the early Georgian period the extreme simplicity of Queen Anne bookcases gave way to treatment of pronounced architectural character, with broken pediments, pilasters and classical cornices as favourite motifs. Batty Langley in the *Treasury of Designs*, 1740, regarded a proper understanding of architecture as essential for cabinet-makers. "'Tis a very great Difficulty," he observed, "to find one in fifty of them that can make a Book-Case etc. indispensably true after any one of the Five Orders without being obliged to a Joiner for to set out the Work, and make his Templet to work by." About 1745 two further developments occurred: the introduction of the bookcase consisting of a centre piece and two wings, and the addition of rococo carving. The most magnificent example of this kind of work – though it was made at a date, 1762, when the Rococo was on the wane – is the very beautiful bookcase made by William Vile for Queen Charlotte. It is in the classical style, but has rococo carving of a superb quality, and altogether it must rank as one of the finest pieces of furniture made in this country.

In the mid-century the architectural character was generally modified. Graceful mahogany glazing bars (Fig. 20) were now used; pediments were sometimes pierced and flanked by fretted galleries; and the break-front was common in the larger examples. The importance which bookcases had attained is clearly shown by the fact that the *Director* of 1762 gives no less than fourteen designs under this heading, all but one having solid bases. Among them are some gothic examples, but their designs are so fanciful that it is unlikely that they were ever actually made, certainly not without a great deal of alteration. On other bookcases of the time the glazing bars, the designs of which varied considerably, were in the gothic taste, but rococo features were also evident in the carving.

Pl. 30 shows a remarkably fine bookcase at Wilton which can be assigned to Chippendale and is one of the best pieces of case furniture made by him in the rococo style. Its date is *c.* 1760. It has a musical trophy in the central section instead of glazing bars. The inlaid stars are noteworthy. They also appear on another bookcase at Wilton (Pl. 27) which lacks the rococo carving, but has the same kind of swan-neck pediment as the former.

Bureaux. The term "bureau" was somewhat loosely used in the early eighteenth century to apply to several kinds of writing furniture. It included what is understood by a bureau today, i.e. the chest of drawers type with a writing-flap. This kind developed on the same general lines as the plainer chest of drawers of the period. But an older type of writing-piece was also being made – the desk on stand, which now had cabriole legs and club or ball-and-claw feet, and in some cases a richly carved underframing. This type seems to have been made for ladies' use, which is further indicated by the fact that some of them were surmounted by a mirror.

The scrutoire was not a very convenient piece of furniture, and it had already been modified into the bureau-cabinet, the bureau in two stages or, as it was then called, the "desk and bookcase". Some fine examples of the latter were produced, either decorated with japan, or in walnut, which remained for a long time the most fashionable wood for bureaux. A notable specimen of a walnut bureau-cabinet of *c.* 1725 is illustrated in Pl. 20B. It has a broken pediment with gilt-metal mounts, carved wood finials and a central figure of Mercury on a plinth. The

mirror is flanked by pilasters which are partly reeded and fluted and have gilt-
metal ionic capitals. The interiors of pieces of this kind were fitted with small
drawers, pigeon-holes, etc., arranged with great ingenuity, and they often contained secret receptacles.

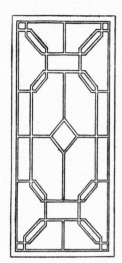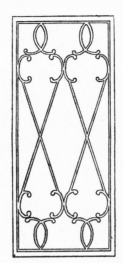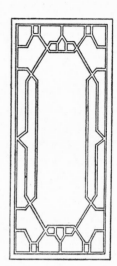

Fig. 20. Bookcase doors designed by T. Chippendale.

During the early Georgian period mahogany bureau-cabinets made for large
houses tended to be of greater size; they were enriched with baroque carving and
had serpentine mouldings around the glazed doors. But about 1750 there was a
return to the less ornate decoration of the earlier pieces, and the main features were
delicate carving, fretted galleries on the cornices and unglazed doors which were
panelled in long, thin mouldings. Several varieties of the "desk and bookcase" appear in the *Director*. In general, they continue on traditional lines but add typical
rococo carving. There is, however, one design in the Chinese taste which shows a
little pagoda crest, a pierced fret gallery and icicle carving. And another innovation which is apparent on some of the designs is the division of the upper part into a
central piece flanked by two smaller wings.

The outstanding example of this kind of furniture is another masterpiece by
Vile – Queen Charlotte's bureau, made in 1761. It has a *bombé* base with beautiful
rococo carving, and an upper part enclosed with delicate latticework in the
Chinese taste, surmounted by a graceful canopy with a crown.

Cabinets. During this period there were several varieties of cabinets used for display purposes, mainly for china or for the collections of curios or "curiosities"
(jewels, coins, medals, etc.), which had been a hobby of the upper classes since the
later seventeenth century. Those cabinets which had glazed upper parts were
very similar to contemporary bookcases in design, so much so, in fact, that it is

E

often impossible to distinguish the exact purpose for which they were intended. On the other hand, there were still examples of the type of cabinet fitted with small drawers and mounted on a stand which had been fashionable in Stuart times. The stands were now made with cabriole legs.

All types of cabinets were influenced by the strong feeling for architectural forms which marked furniture of this kind in the second quarter of the century, but after 1750 this treatment was modified. Chippendale presented designs for both cabinets and china cases in the prevailing styles, with a preference, which was most clearly and understandably discernible in the china cases, for the Chinese taste. Many of these pieces were japanned. There was also much free blending of Chinese and rococo decoration. Pl. 29A shows how delicately, on occasions, this could be done, and it further illustrates one of the many kinds of combined pieces – in this case a cabinet and writing-table – which were made at the time. Small hanging cabinets for displaying china were also popular; they often had fretwork doors and sides.

An example of the enclosed cabinet on stand is Queen Charlotte's jewel cabinet supplied by Vile and Cobb in 1761. It is made of mahogany, with rich rococo carving, inlays of ivory, and veneers of various choice woods, all executed with consummate skill.

Mirrors. Considerable changes occurred in the design of mirrors at this time, particularly in that of pier-glasses, for their prominent position on the wall between the windows in reception-rooms called for special decorative treatment. Three main trends can be distinguished. Until about 1725 elegant mirrors of carved and gilt wood and gesso were fashionable. A fine example is shown in Pl. 20A. Here the gilt gesso frame, five feet four inches high, has a shaped and scrolled cresting ornamented with a shell, and a shaped base. Mirrors of this kind usually had candle-branches attached to the base, as had the smaller hanging mirrors of the same period. The latter were generally square in shape and had similar gesso ornament of shells, scrolls and eagles' heads, but some simple and attractive ones were made in walnut with shaped crests which contained a central gilt decoration.

After about 1725 pier-glasses acquired an architectural character. The moulded frames were surmounted by a broken pediment which centred in a shell, plinth or cartouche; the sides were often enriched with floral ornament or draperies; and the bases were either curved, with a shell or similar decoration, or were straight and had a classical motif such as the Vitruvian scroll or the egg-and-dart. The usual materials were gilt soft woods and gesso, or walnut and mahogany veneers with gilt mouldings and ornament. In larger houses, where the whole of the decoration of the interior was directed by the architect, the mouldings of pier-glasses often matched those on the window architraves, doorways and cornices, and console tables were specially designed to harmonize with the mirrors beneath which they stood.

After 1745 this architectural form gave way to the rococo taste which found in gilt mirror-frames perhaps its freest expression. C scrolls gradually replaced straight lines until at length highly ornamental open-work carving was the mode. Intricate arrangements of scrolls, curling leaves and *coquillage* were mingled with chinoiseries – mandarins, birds, icicles, pagodas, etc. Chippendale exploited the

Fig. 22. (*above*) Hoop-back Windsor chair, first half of the eighteenth century.

Fig. 21. (*left*) Upper portion of long-case clock, showing dome and finials, *c.* 1725.

new trends to the full. Two other prominent contemporary designers of mirrors in this style were Lock and Thomas Johnson, but some of the latter's designs were so extravagant as to be impracticable.

In Pl. 21, which illustrates some typical forms of the decoration employed by Chippendale, the fusion of styles is exemplified by the crest of *coquillage* surmounted by a bird. This mirror is of interest because an overmantel mirror in the earlier architectural style is reflected in it; the two mirrors thus show the changes which had occurred during the second quarter of the century. Overmantel mirrors were frequently divided into compartments and a number of them had brackets for displaying china. The carving of mirror frames had now become a highly special-ized craft. "This business," wrote Collyer in 1761, "which has lately been carried to great perfection, requires much ingenuity, a lively and elegant fancy, skill in drawing with great neatness foliages, fruit, flowers, birds, heads, etc., a good eye, and a steady hand."[1] Good carvers were rated highly and were among the best paid of the London craftsmen.

Clock-cases. Clocks as pieces of furniture allied the crafts of the clock-maker and of the case-maker. Both these crafts had reached a very high standard in the late seventeenth century, and this was maintained under the first two Georges. For the decoration of long-case clocks marquetry went out of fashion and the best cases were decorated with finely figured walnut veneers or with japan. Walnut cases show the figure to great advantage, and if they seem somewhat plainer than the intricate marquetry pieces of the preceding period, this really accentuates their elegant proportions and excellent workmanship. Cases tended to increase in height as rooms became larger. The clock dials had arched tops decorated with brasswork and were surmounted by arched hoods completed with domes and finials. Carving was seldom employed, and then only for minor details such as crestings, finials and, more rarely still, feet; for all these details soft woods were used, either stained to match the walnut, or gilded.

Japanned long-case clocks, with various forms of oriental designs (Fig. 21), enjoyed great popularity during this period. The more usual background colours were green, black, red and blue, but yellow and scarlet were also found. Bright colours were used for the cases exported to what was then called the South Europe and Mediterranean trade – Spain, Portugal, Italy and Turkey – where there was a brisk demand for English clocks and watches.

For some twenty years after 1740 long-case clocks were less popular than the smaller bracket or table clocks, and the wall variety known as cartel clocks. One reason for this was that smaller clocks were more suitable for the elaborate carving and decoration of the rococo phase. Cartel clocks were made of soft woods carved and gilt; for bracket clocks, however, mahogany was coming into general use. The *Director* has illustrations of bracket clocks in both the rococo and Chinese tastes, and both the carving and the details like pagoda domes and fretwork show that the traditional designs of these clocks had now been considerably modified. When, about 1755, the long-case clocks began to return to favour, close-grained mahogany was chiefly employed, enriched with carving and fretwork, and some of the graceful proportions of the earlier cases were lost, for the bodies tended to become shorter and broader.

Country furniture. The kind of furniture which could be found in villages and hamlets depended on many variable factors among which, to name but a few, one might put the nearness to a town or port, the skill of the local craftsmen, and the poverty or prosperity of the community concerned. In isolated areas, such as Devon and Cornwall, the furniture in cottages seems to have been both scanty and

[1] *Parent's and Guardian's Directory*, by J. Collyer, 1761.

primitive, consisting of a table, chairs (or, more likely, a form and stools), a chest and perhaps a bedstead. This state of affairs was confirmed at a much later date by Louis Simond's description of the interiors of Devon cottages during his travels in England in 1810–11.[1] But elsewhere cottages and farm-houses could have more comfortable equipment. In most villages the joiner supplied, besides tables, chairs, chests and beds, such pieces as settles, hanging and corner cupboards and dressers. The last-named deserve special mention. Their prototypes had been found in the halls of medieval houses and had continued to be fashionable until the seventeenth century, when they were relegated to the kitchen and replaced by walnut and later mahogany side-tables. About 1750 oak cottage dressers, which had resembled long tables with cupboards, often had an upper stage of shelves to display earthenware and pewter. Occasionally there were details of ornament and construction which were influenced by fashionable furniture, but such modifications were retained long after they had gone out of fashion in London. Cabriole legs, for instance, were adapted to dressers during this period and continued in use until the end of the century.

Contemporary inventories of cottage furniture were so rare that special interest attaches to one which was drawn up in 1768 by the parish authorities of New Brentford, Middlesex. It shows that the furniture which had been in the possession of the occupier – he was described as a labourer, but his effects indicate that he was of a higher status, probably an artisan or craftsman – provided more than a modest degree of comfort. The bedroom furniture included feather beds and bolsters, "a four post Bedstead with Green Harrateen Furniture", and "a half Tester turn up Bedstead with Green Furniture". There were five tables, two of the type described as "wainscott Dining Table", four cane and five rush-bottomed chairs, and "a leather Covered Elbow chair". Also on the list were "a Deal Cloths Chest ... a wainscott Chest with Drawers veneered in Front ... a Mahogany Tea Chest ... eight Prints ... two small looking glasses". There was a certain amount of old furniture in the garret.[2]

Though most country furniture was made locally, some cottages had articles which came from London. Defoe wrote the following (probably exaggerated) account in 1726: "it is scarce credible to how many counties of England, and how remote, the furniture of but a mean house must send them ... the chairs, if of cane, are made at London; the ordinary matted chairs, perhaps in the place where they live .... Tables, chests of drawers etc. made at London; as also looking-glass."[3] Such goods would be distributed from the ports in the south and east which could be readily reached in the coasting trade from London.

[1] *Journal of a Tour & Residence in Great Britain*, 1810–11, by L. Simond, 1817.
[2] Middlesex Sessions Books, (Middlesex Guildhall), No. 1229, 1768.
[3] *The Complete English Tradesman*, by D. Defoe, 1726.

LATE GEORGIAN

FEW students of furniture history would quarrel with the statement that the half century or so after 1760 marked the zenith of English cabinet-making. During this period the closest harmony existed between the work of the architect and that of the furniture-maker, and the skill of the craftsman was at its highest. English furniture in the neo-classical style set a European fashion, and equalled in technique the best work of the great French cabinet-makers, two facts which give point to Hepplewhite's statement in 1788 that "English taste and workmanship have, of late years, been much sought for by surrounding nations".

For the whole of this period furniture-making was carried on by the traditional methods of the craftsman, although wood-working machinery had been patented by Sir Samuel Bentham in the 1790's. There was, however, no simple pattern in the organization of the industry; on the contrary, since early Georgian times almost every type of industrial organization had been developing, especially in the towns, and above all, in London. This diversity is explained by the growth of specialization and the extent of the market. The village craftsman represented the unspecialized workman because his market was so limited. "A country carpenter", wrote Adam Smith in 1776, "deals in every kind of work that is made of wood . . . (he) is not only a carpenter, but a joiner, a cabinet-maker and even a carver in wood." This was in marked contrast with the specialization of the town craftsmen, among whom could be found minute sub-divisions of trades. In London a cabinet-maker – to take only one class of craftsman as an example – might mean one of several things: a craftsman-shopkeeper who was responsible for the making on his own premises of the furniture which he sold to the public; or a capitalist-shop-keeper who was a dealer only, retailing furniture which he bought from outside craftsmen, and sometimes supplying it to other dealers for sale in different parts of the country and overseas; or a working master who was not a shopkeeper, but had his own workshop where he made furniture, or parts of it, for the shops and other craftsmen; or, finally, one of the numerous journeymen who either worked at home as outworkers by the piece for the shops and masters, or were wage-earners in other craftsmen's workshops. These divisions were subject to endless variations as one merged into the other.

The pre-eminence of London. It is well to emphasize the predominant position of London, not only in the size of the market and the physical output of furniture – the capital's population was a million at the census of 1811, when Manchester's, then the next largest city, was some 130,000 – but also in its leadership in styles and techniques. There were, of course, plenty of excellent craftsmen in the main provincial towns, but they looked to the capital for the latest furniture fashions, and one of the chief functions of the many design books which emanated from London in this period was to spread these new ideas (to quote Hepplewhite again) "to many of our own Countrymen and Artizans whose distance from the Metropolis makes even an imperfect knowledge of its improvements acquired with much trouble and expense". Ever since Defoe's day there had been a noticeable tendency for some London furniture shops to grow in size. In the second half of the eighteenth century St Paul's Churchyard began to lose some, but by no means all, of its reputation as the main centre for high-quality furniture, for many of the fashionable shops were now to be found in the Covent Garden, St Martin's Lane and Long Acre district, and in Soho, Old and New Bond Street, Oxford Street and Tottenham Court Road, where they were close to the newer residential areas. Some shops where the furniture was made on the premises under the control of a craftsman were of a large size and resembled in a way a departmental store. Such, for example, was the well-known shop of George Seddon in Aldersgate Street (not, it will be noted, in one of the fashionable areas just mentioned), which was described by a German visitor, Sophie von la Roche, in 1786 as a large building with six wings employing "four hundred apprentices (i.e. journeymen) on any work connected with the making of furniture".[1] The stock of the firm, including carpets, wood and mirrors (which were cast and cut in the basement) was valued at nearly £119,000 in 1789, shortly after the above description was written.

Even in the case of the smaller shops the nature of the work must have made the craftsmen in charge more business men than craftsmen. Chippendale, for instance, travelled so much about the country to attend to customer's requirements, which often included the fitting up of a whole house, that he could not possibly have had time to see personally to the work being carried out in his workshop. This means that much of the fine furniture which came from the better-known shops was made, not by the craftsman whose name appeared on the bill, but by the foreman and band of highly-skilled, unknown workmen – carvers, inlayers, chair-makers, upholsterers, etc. – to whom the real credit should go.

Little is known in detail of the other kinds of shops which were run by dealers, but it is clear that there were very many of them in London doing a considerable business. Mortimer's *Universal Director* of 1763, which was the first London directory to classify trades, stated that its list of cabinet-makers "contains only such as either work themselves, or employ workmen under their direction; and that not one of those numerous Cabinet Warehouses which sell ready-made Furniture

[1] *Sophie in London*, 1786 (trans. by C. Williams, 1933).

bought of the real artist, is to be met with in this work". The general scope of the work of these dealers is illustrated by the handbill of Wilkinson & Sons who kept a "Cabinet, Upholstery, Carpet and Looking-Glass Warehouse" in Cheapside. This bill (in the Guildhall Collection, dated 1779) advertises that the shop "keeps ready made in the most genteel taste" a very wide range of goods which are given in detail, including such items as "library, writing, ladies' dressing, Pembroke, dining, card and tea tables" and "cabriole, japand, dyed and Windsor chairs". The statement concludes: "N.B. Merchants, Captains and others may be supplied with the above Goods at the most Reasonable Rates," indicating that these shops were one of the channels through which furniture and upholstery were sent from London to distant parts of the country and overseas.

London cabinet-ware exports reached all parts of the world with which we had trading relations, foreign countries as well as British colonies. In 1800 the total value of British furniture exports (mainly from London) was well over £38,000 in the official Customs returns, even though we were then at war with France; and this figure was certainly an understatement, for the real value was probably well above that given, and did not include all the furniture taken out of the country by emigrants, or the goods traded privately to India by the officials of the East India Company. It was not, of course, only dealers who sent goods abroad, for furniture from good craftsmen's shops is known to have gone to the rich planter classes in the West Indies and to North America where it was imported by rich Americans or by the cabinet-makers to copy and re-sell. This trade continued to flourish well into the nineteenth century until it was curtailed by the increasingly heavy duties on imported timber. The English furniture industry in the Georgian period can never be divorced from its world-wide setting.

The Adam style. For a quarter of a century after 1760 the great name in furniture design was Robert Adam (1728–92). In place of the medley of styles of the early Chippendale period – the rococo, gothic and Chinese, which were in reality variations on the same theme – he designed in the neo-classical style, and his furniture was an essential part of his scheme of treating the decoration of a house, inside and out, as a harmonious whole. In his own words in the preface to *The Works in Architecture* in 1773 he was greatly inspired by "the grotesque . . . that beautiful light style of ornament used by the ancient Romans in the decoration of their palaces, baths and villas. . . . This classical style of ornament, by far the most perfect that has ever appeared for inside decorations . . . requires not only fancy and imagination in the composition, but taste and judgement in the application; and when these are happily combined, this gay and elegant mode is capable of inimitable beauties." Adam's furniture in this style employed a variety of classical motifs carried out with great delicacy; among them were festoons of husks, paterae, the honeysuckle, ram's heads, vases, urns, the acanthus leaf, and medallions (Pls. 34C, 35B, 36A). These could be found carved in low relief in the solid, or, perhaps at their best, in the fine inlaid work, for which many choice coloured woods were used, particularly satinwood. Adam designed for rich patrons and the furniture was made by leading craftsmen, including Chippendale at Kenwood, Harewood House, Nostell Priory, Mersham Hatch and elsewhere, France and Beckwith at Kenwood, Linnell at Osterley, and Norman at Moor Park. Among the earliest furniture Adam is known to have designed was some for Queen Charlotte, and her beautiful bed, which originally stood in the Queen's House, now Buckingham Palace, can be seen today in the Public Dining Room at Hampton Court.

The new style did not completely sweep away the Chinese and gothic modes, which still found a certain amount of favour; and French-style furniture continued to enjoy a vogue among the upper classes. Many cabinet-makers imported French pieces to sell to their clients or to copy – Chippendale was fined by the Customs in 1769 for alleged under-valuation of chairs which he had imported from France – and Adam complied with the demand by designing pieces, particularly uphol-stered chairs, with a distinctly French flavour. But his new classical style was catching on in the 1760's. "The light and elegant ornaments," wrote Sir John Soane in the early nineteenth century, ". . . were soon applied in designs for Chairs Tables, Carpets, and in every other species of Furniture. To Mr Adam's taste in the Ornaments of his Buildings and Furniture we stand indebted, in-as-much as Manufacturers of every kind felt, as it were, the electric power of this Revolution in art."[1]

Holland and the Regency style. The inevitable reaction against the Adam style set in before the end of the century, and the changes were heralded by the work of the gifted architect and designer, Henry Holland (1745–1806). Unlike other architects, he did not make a tour of classical sites abroad, and this probably made him more receptive to new trends, especially from France, for he was also closely connected with the Whig coterie which surrounded the Prince of Wales (the future Regent and George IV), and he shared their enthusiasm for French ideas. At first he followed a modified Adam style, but later branched out into the English version of what came to be known as the French "Directoire" style. He stressed the close adaptation of Græco-Roman forms of decoration, and to obtain accuracy of detail he sent his draughtsman, C. H. Tatham, to Rome in 1794 to study antique classical ornament at first hand. Holland's best-known furniture designs were carried out for the Prince of Wales at Carlton House from 1784 (some of this furniture is now at Buckingham Palace), and for Samuel Whitbread at Southill from 1795. The strength of French influence is shown by the fact that Holland employed French craftsmen at both places.[2]

This new classic style has been given the general name of "Regency". So far as

---

[1] Sir J. Soane, *Lectures on Architecture*, 1809–36 (ed. A. T. Bolton, 1929).

[2] For Holland's furniture see D. Stroud, *Henry Holland*, 1950, and F. Watson's chapter in *Southill: a Regency House*, 1951.

furniture is concerned, this must remain a somewhat vague and elastic term, by no means coinciding with the actual political limits of the Regency, for while the latter lasted from 1811 to 1820, the changes in design, as has been shown, were clearly evident before the close of the preceding century. In fact, it was in 1785 that Horace Walpole saw Holland's work at Carlton House and wrote his well-known comment: "How sick one shall be after this chaste place, of Mr. Adam's gingerbread and sippets of embroidery!" We must allow that Walpole was not a friendly critic of Adam's work, but his sentiments were shared by others after the turn of the century. In 1808, for instance, C. A. Busby described Adam as "a mannerist" and wrote: "This ebullition of a false taste having now subsided, the latter (i.e. Adam) is considered only as an Artist of enterprize and ability."[1] Soane's appreciation of Adam, already quoted, was noteworthy at a time when the latter's style was considered outmoded.

Holland had a sure grasp of style, and however much he was influenced by French designs, he never fell into the habit of merely copying them, but gave them an unmistakable English twist. He favoured the use of rosewood with resplendent ormolu mounts, marble tops to chiffoniers, tapered, gilded and fluted pillars, lion's legs on smaller tables, and round tops for larger tables mounted on a massive pedestal or monopodium. He also designed chairs and settees at Southill in imitation bamboo, in the Chinese fashion, and at times used Egyptian motifs, such as the lotus leaf, another characteristic of the Regency style.

After Holland. While Holland was alive this new treatment was kept under control, but after his death in 1806 it began to degenerate into a somewhat narrow archaeological approach which resulted in very close copies of classical furtniture, Egyptian, Greek and Roman. The pioneer of this new interpretation, which was at first founded on sound scholarship, was Thomas Hope (1769–1831), a rich banker and collector of antiques, who had had some training as an architect. In 1807 he published his *Household Furniture and Interior Decoration* in which he aimed, as he wrote in the Introduction, at "that breadth and repose of surface, that distinctness and contrast of outline, that opposition of plain and enriched parts, that harmony and significance of accessories . . . which are calculated to afford to the eye and mind the most lively, most permanent and most unfading enjoyment". He spoke of the "association of all the elegancies of antique forms and ornaments with all the requisites of modern customs and habits". It is not difficult to understand how designers of the time who lacked Hope's scholarly knowledge merely imitated ancient furniture, often in a lifeless way, and these results could be seen at the very end of the period under review.

The ideas behind all these changes in design after about 1785 were well expressed by Archibald Alison in his *Essays on the Nature and Principles of Taste*, which were first published in 1790 and reached their sixth edition in 1825. He stressed the

[1] C. A. Busby, *A Series of Designs for Villas & Country Houses*, 1808.

importance of delicacy and straight lines: "All Furniture . . . is Beautiful in proportion to its quantity of Matter, or the Fineness or Delicacy of it. Strong and Massy Furniture is everywhere vulgar and unpleasing . . . progress terminates in that last degree of Delicacy and even of Fragility, which is consistent either with the nature of the Workmanship or the preservation of the Subject." The models should be "the Forms of Grecian or Roman Furniture . . . in scarcely any of them is the winding or serpentine Form observed; . . . on the contrary, the lightest and most beautiful of them are almost universally distinguished by straight or angular Lines". All this is typical of what we call Sheraton style furniture. Alison justified the Chinese and gothic styles by the ideas with which they were associated. For example, Chinese furniture, "however fantastic and uncouth the Forms in reality were . . . brought to mind those images of Eastern magnificence and splendour of which we have heard so much". Similarly, with regard to the gothic taste, "this slight association was sufficient to give Beauty to such Forms, because it led to ideas of Gothic manners and adventure".

The design books. The architect-designers worked for a relatively small clientele and designed furniture of high quality. The translation of their styles into general furniture, including quite humble pieces, was accomplished by the authors of design books which were intended, as Hepplewhite wrote, to be "useful to the mechanic and serviceable to the gentleman". Chippendale's *Director* of 1754 had been the first of such furniture catalogues to be published by a cabinet-maker and not by a builder, artist or architect, and it was followed by many others. At the end of the decade 1760–70 the neo-classical style began to appear in such publications. At first the mid-century fashions set by Chippendale, the third edition of whose *Director* appeared in 1762, were continued in Ince and Mayhew's *Universal System of Household Furniture* (1759–63) and in various works by Matthias Lock, Robert Manwaring (who specialized in chair designs) and others. But in 1769 Lock, who was a carver as well as designer, and had been the pioneer of the Rococo in England, showed his versatility by publishing two works, the *New Book of Pier Frames* and the *New Book of Foliage* which contained the first engraved designs of furniture in the Adam style. What really popularized the new mode, however, was Hepplewhite's *Guide* of 1788, published two years after the author's death. With nearly 300 designs, covering all kinds of furniture, it illustrated admirably how the application of Adam's principles, "the latest or most prevailing fashion", could "unite elegance and utility, and blend the useful with the agreeable". Designs similar to Hepplewhite's appeared in the *Cabinet-Makers' London Book of Prices*, also published in 1788; many of the plates for this had been designed by Thomas Shearer, who re-issued them under his own name as *Designs for Household Furniture* in the same year.

The changes at the end of the century were interpreted in Thomas Sheraton's famous *Drawing Book*, published in parts between 1791–4. It reflected the emphasis on light and delicate furniture, the making of which required a very high standard of skill from the craftsmen; in fact, the furniture of this particular period can properly be considered among the most technically perfect ever made in this country. Sheraton also published a *Cabinet Dictionary* in 1803, and the first volume of an unfinished *Encyclopaedia* in 1805. The latter, however, showed signs of the deterioration which was then beginning to mark furniture design. Hope's publication of 1807, already referred to, differed from the others in that it was not the work of a craftsman. His principles were generally applied to furniture in 1808 by George Smith, a cabinet-maker, in his *Household Furniture*. Smith did not possess Hope's scholarship, and he lost some of the spirit in which Hope's interpretations were made.

Leading cabinet-makers. Some of these designers were also craftsmen of great repute in their own day, but this by no means applied to all of them. Among the names in the above list, those of Chippendale, Hepplewhite and Sheraton are household words, and will remain so. Their fame, however, is due to their well-advertised skill as designers and to the very convenient way in which their names can label the furniture of their period, rather than to their supremacy as craftsmen. Chippendale was certainly responsible for fine pieces, but he had no royal appointment and it is a curious fact that his best work was done, not in the styles of his own *Director*, but in the quite different Adam style. Hepplewhite does not seem to have enjoyed any great reputation as a furniture-maker. As for Sheraton, who died in poverty, there is no evidence that he ever had a workshop of his own.

Many contemporary craftsmen of outstanding worth have been unfairly overshadowed by these designers. In the 'sixties flourished the great partnership of William Vile and John Cobb; Vile, indeed, did work in the rococo style in its later phase here which surpassed that of Chippendale. When the neo-classical style took root, outstanding pieces, in addition to Chippendale's (already noted), were produced by William Gates and John Linnell. At the end of the century and just after, prominent names were those of William Marsh, Thomas Tatham (these last two were partners for a time), Thomas Chippendale the younger and George Oakley. On the other hand, among those who published design books we find that the partners Ince and Mayhew ranked highly as craftsmen, and so did George Smith, who had royal appointments in the early nineteenth century. Two long-lived firms, those of Gillow and Seddon, were also widely known throughout this period.

Decoration. Several new forms of decoration, and revivals of older ones, appeared on furniture during this period. And one traditional decorative craft, that of the carver, though strongly evident for most of the period, was decaying in the early nineteenth century. In 1761 J. Collyer described carvers as "ingenious men . . . never out of business", but in 1813, T. Martin, author of *The Circle of the Mechanical*

Arts, wrote thus: "Carving in wood has long been in the background, as a branch of the arts. . . . There are now only eleven master carvers in London, and about sixty journeymen (though at one time there were six hundred); many of the latter are now very old. They make no shew of their work, and live in private houses."

One feature of the Adam style was the revival of marquetry in the form of fine inlaid work (Pls. 34C, 38C). This was similar in technique to the marquetry of the walnut period, but differed from it in emphasizing classical decoration. Towards 1800 this kind of decoration gradually gave way to the simpler form of "stringing", by which a thin line of wood or, more particularly at the end of this period, brass, was inlaid on the furniture (Pls. 33B, 38A). This change, and the reasons for it, was thus described by Sheraton in 1803: – "Inlaying, in cabinet-making, was much in use between twenty and thirty years back; but was soon laid aside, as a very expensive mode of ornamenting furniture, as well as being subject to speedy decay. The present mode of inlaying with brass, is most durable and looks well let into black woods of any kind." This brass work is a characteristic feature of furniture at the turn of the century, and set off the dark glossy and striped woods which became popular after the decay of carving and inlay.

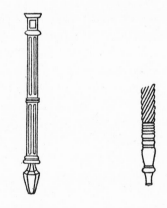

Fig. 23. Turned and reeded chair-leg.   Fig. 24. Spiral twist chair-leg.

There were new developments in metal mounts. When Matthew Boulton, the industrial pioneer and partner of James Watt, opened his famous factory at Soho, near Birmingham, in 1762, he began to manufacture ormolu mounts, finely chased and of a rich, golden colour. Boulton always aimed at a high artistic standard in his products, and was influenced by Adam's work. Samuel Smiles, in his life of Boulton and Watt, quotes Lord Shelburne as writing to Adam that "he (i.e. Boulton) is very desirous of cultivating Mr Adam's taste in his productions". In the last quarter of the century a new method of manufacturing backplates for drawer handles came into use. In 1777 two Birmingham brass-founders, John Marston and Samuel Bellamy, improved upon John Pickering's invention of 1769 by patenting a method of stamping ornaments on plated metal for cabinet furniture.[1] The plates of brass were moulded by dies, and were usually circular, oval or octagonal in shape (Pl. 34B). About 1800 another form of handle appeared: small brass knobs, many in the shape of a lion's head with a ring through the mouth. Turned mahogany knobs were also used (Pl. 35A).

[1] Patent Office Library, Old Series of Abridgements of Specifications, Class 39, Furniture & Upholstery, 1620–1866 (1869).

The vogue for lighter and more delicate furniture led to a revival of three fashionable late seventeenth-century features which had undergone a more or less total eclipse: turning, cane work, and japanning. Turned legs on chairs and tables, of slender proportions and often fluted, were in great favour (Pls. 32C and D, 34B). Sheraton also shows turned and reeded legs (Fig. 23) on some of his pieces, and about 1800 spiral-twisted turning could be found on chair legs and backs (Fig. 24), and as columns at the corners of chests of drawers. As for cane work and japanning, these went together, as Sheraton himself pointed out: "Caning cabinet work is now more in use than it was ever known to be at any former period. About thirty years since, it was quite gone out of fashion. . . . But on the revival of japanning furniture it began to be gradually brought into use, and to a state of improvement". This later method of japanning, however, was much inferior to the original process; it was merely paint and varnish, even in the case of the well-known bedroom suite for Garrick at Hampton. At the end of the century it was often used for brightly coloured patterns (Pl. 32D).

Woods: mahogany. The extensive character of British trade enabled the cabinet-makers of the later Georgian period to take their pick of the world's choicest furniture woods. The outstanding wood was mahogany from the West Indies and Central America, and the most important event in the history of the mahogany trade was the Act of 1721 (see page 56) which freed timbers grown in the British plantations in America (including the West Indies) from their former heavy import duties. In 1750 the value of imported mahogany, which included wood smuggled from Spanish colonies via Jamaica to avoid the duties on foreign timbers, was nearly £30,000, compared with £221 in 1721. So important had the trade become that in 1770 the Government, at the instigation of Customs officials, passed another Act (11 Geo. III, c. 41) extending this freedom from duty to all American timbers, foreign and British alike, as mahogany – so ran the preamble of the Act – had "become very useful and necessary to cabinet-makers" and further supplies would encourage increased exports of furniture from Britain. In 1792 the import value was £79,554, and in 1800, despite the war with France and the re-imposition of duties, £77,744. The quantity represented by these last two sums was in each case well over 7,000 tons. After about 1750 the Cuban variety of mahogany, easier to work, richly coloured, and often with a range of beautiful figures (among them "fiddle-backs", "roes", and "curls") began to replace the earlier San Domingo variety, which was harder and denser, and had little figure. In the later part of the century mahogany from Honduras (often called "baywood") was popular; it was lighter in both colour and weight, and was sometimes used as a carcase for Cuban veneers, though for this purpose red deal, imported from North America, was commonly employed. In the figures quoted for import values in 1792 Honduras mahogany accounted for nearly £46,000 of the total, and in Sheraton's day it was "the principal kind of mahogany in use among cabinet-makers".

Satinwood and rosewood. Towards the end of the century two other woods were in demand for the best quality furniture: satinwood and rosewood. Satinwood was imported from both the West and East Indies, and its light yellow colour and fine figure, which showed up beautifully under polish, made it ideal for the delicate pieces of the period. It was used mainly as a veneer on case furniture (Pl. 38c), though some work in the solid (chairs and tables) was evident about 1800. Rosewood was particularly important after 1800; heavy, dense, and marked with dark streaks, it set the current fashion for dark, glossy woods, and its use was encouraged by the opening of direct trade with South America, where the chief source of supply was Brazil, during the Napoleonic Wars. It would be incorrect to assume that these woods supplanted each other in turn, as mahogany had supplanted walnut; it would be more accurate to say that one was more fashionable than the others at particular times, for fine furniture. In general terms it may be said that towards the end of this period mahogany was used for the best furniture in dining-rooms, bedrooms and libraries, and satinwood and rosewood in drawing-

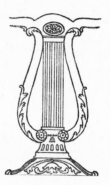 

Fig. 25. Lyre back of chair.   Fig. 26. Prince of Wales feather back of chair.

rooms and boudoirs. But it can be noted that in 1810 cabinet-makers were still defined in *Crosby's Pocket Dictionary* as "workers in mahogany and other fine woods".

Other woods. Many timbers besides those mentioned were in demand for their colour or figure. Fustic, long imported from the West Indies for dyeing, enjoyed a temporary popularity in cabinet work after about 1770 because of its yellow colour but it fell into disuse when it was found to fade to a dead brownish hue. Various beautiful shades of brown and red, light and dark, were provided by exotic woods like calamander from Ceylon, coromandel from India, thuya from Africa, kingwood, partridge wood, purple wood, zebra wood and tulip wood all from Brazil, and amboyna from the West Indies. All these could be found as veneers or decorative bandings. It was the great demand for veneers with striped figure which explains the particular use of many of these woods after 1800. Cheaper foreign woods which were imported included red cedar from North and Central America for boxes and drawer linings, and red deal from North America which, after 1750, began to replace yellow deal from the Baltic for carcase work.

English timbers were used considerably by leading cabinet-makers, and were by no means confined, as is sometimes supposed, to country craftsmen. Some native woods resembled the more expensive foreign varieties. Suitably figured pieces of birch and chestnut, for instance, could be used as substitutes for satinwood; acacia was used instead of tulip wood; and ebony, which had been imported since the sixteenth century for its black colour, was not now in such demand, since it could be imitated by staining close-grained woods like pear and willow for the "ebonized" stringing on Regency pieces. Sycamore, stained to give a greenish-grey colour, and known as silver-wood or harewood, was often used as a veneer on late eighteenth-century work. Without such refinements, these and other native woods were found on the simple but attractive furniture made by country craftsmen or by cabinet-makers in the smaller towns, in imitation of better quality work. For painted furniture beech was usually employed, but plane was often substituted for this in country areas. And in the traditional craft of Windsor chair-making elm for the seat, beech or ash for the spindles, and yew for the frame continued to be frequently used.

Fashionable furniture: chairs. Under Adam's influence chairs were lighter and more graceful than those of the rococo period. Characteristic features were straight legs which tapered from knee blocks at the level of the seat rail to feet ending on small plinths, delicate classical motifs carved, inlaid, or painted, and a graceful outline for the backs. The latter had many variations; oval, shield and heart shapes became fashionable, but the rectilinear form was also in use, as, for example, on some early specimens of about 1775 which had lyre-shaped splats (Fig. 25). Where carving was employed it usually took the form of delicate channelling or fluting on the back frame, carved oval paterae on the knee blocks, fluting on the tapered legs, and continuous moulding along the seat edge. Adam's upholstered chairs closely followed French models, and he used beautiful materials like brocades and tapestries for upholstering both backs (which were oval in shape) and seats. The latter were overstuffed, but showed the lower part of the seat frames clear, and these were often decorated with gadrooning. Sometimes chairs of this kind had serpentine-curved front legs ending on scroll feet, the last version of the cabriole leg, and had arms with padded tops, covered with the same material as backs and seats (Pl. 37).

As can be expected, oval, shield and heart shapes figured prominently on the chair designs in Hepplewhite's *Guide*, and in many cases the splats were not connected with the back of the seats. Hepplewhite's name is particularly associated with the shield back and the familiar Prince of Wales' feathers (Fig. 26), but he designed many other fillings for his backs, including leaves, drapery, wheat-ears, vases and honeysuckle, and he by no means neglected rectilinear backs. The legs were generally of square section and tapered slightly to plinth feet. Many of the supports of the arms of both Adam and Hepplewhite chairs had a common feature in that they did not rise from the side rails of the seat, but continued from the front legs to just above the seat, and then swept backwards in a pronounced curve to straighten out at the arm-rests, which joined the back of the chair about half-way up. (For these details see Pls. 32A and B.)

A great variety of designs was found on chairs of the Sheraton style, but the emphasis was decidedly on backs of rectangular shape. Some cresting rails were turned; others were wide and flat and overran the uprights, and were curved for the sitter's back – this was a novel design very characteristic of chairs of about 1800. The backs were left as open as possible; the fillings took many forms – sometimes a single cross rail, or, when splats were used, trellis bars, pierced circles between pairs of bars, or a panel of cane set in a small frame. Painted chairs usually had bright designs on a black background, turned legs, and seats of cane. A feature

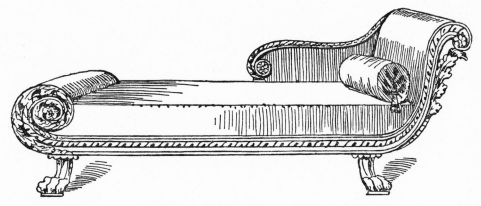

Fig. 27. Late eighteenth-century couch.

of front legs was that they were often shaped in concave curves and tapered gradually to the floor without any special foot design. It was another characteristic of chairs of this time that their arms swept up in a pronounced S-curve to join the back uprights close to the cresting rail. Stringing, the delicate, thin lines of wood or brass, could be found on the broad types of cresting rails. In general, this period was distinguished for the delicacy of its chair design, but the lightness was soon to be lost in the heavier decoration of the Regency style. (Sheraton chairs, Pls. 32C and D.)

Settees followed the same main trends as chairs; they must, however, be carefully distinguished from sofas or couches which were popular at the time. Settees were extensions of armchairs, while couches were descendants of day-beds, and were used for reclining. The couch of classical design figured very prominently in the Regency period (Fig. 27).

Chests of drawers, commodes, tallboys. Chests of drawers of the old plain rectangular form continued to be made after 1760, but often with five or six drawers, and thus somewhat taller than the earlier ones. Many were made of mahogany, either solid or veneered; in the latter case, it was usual to have a carcase of red deal and drawer linings of oak. A general feature of this type was the

F

cock bead round the drawer edge; in fact, this form of moulding, which was introduced during the walnut period, was almost exclusively used throughout the century after about 1745. Some low chests of drawers had the top drawer hinged at the bottom so that it could be opened as a writing flap, and the drawer itself could be pulled forwards. This construction succeeded the writing slide which had been fitted above the top drawer of many chests in the earlier part of the century, and which was pulled out with small loop handles. After 1770 French influence could be seen on these plainer pieces in the form of a delicate outward curving of the feet, instead of the square bracket feet.

But it was in the development of commodes that the French taste was most marked. These pieces stood in reception rooms or the best bedrooms and were often elaborately decorated. Pl. 33A shows a remarkably fine specimen of this kind of about 1765. In the Adam period outstanding examples were made of satinwood inlaid with various woods and decorated with a variety of classical motifs, or with

Fig. 28. Apron piece of bow-fronted chest of drawers.

figures and scenes from classical mythology, all worked with the greatest skill. Among them is the famous "Diana and Minerva" commode supplied by Chippendale, almost certainly to Adam's design, for Harewood House in November, 1773. The inlay work on this piece is superb, particularly on the concave surface of the knee-hole, and the veneers, which are still in excellent condition, illustrate the extraordinary care with which cabinet-makers chose their woods for work of this kind.

After 1775 many chests of drawers were bow- or serpentine-fronted (Fig. 28). Reeded quarter columns were sometimes found on the front corners, and spirally turned feet were fashionable. Stringing in wood or brass was used as a decoration for drawer fronts in the Sheraton period, another distinctive feature of which was the exceptionally wide frieze above the top drawer.

Tallboys or chests-on-chests continued to follow the main developments of the plainer chests of drawers, but they were gradually going out of fashion in the later part of the eighteenth century owing to the inconvenient height of the upper drawers. In the final phase, some bow-fronted ones were made.

Sideboards. One interesting development in this period was the emergence of the sideboard, and credit for this new piece is now generally given to Robert Adam.

"A side Board table in the dining-room" appears among Adam's designs for Ken-wood in the *Works in Architecture* of 1773. This shows the first stage in the arrange-ment of the sideboard – a side table flanked by two detached pedestal cupboards supporting urns (Pl. 34c). Later the two pedestals were joined directly to the table to form one complete unit. The urns were retained and were used as knife boxes, and drawers were fitted to the table and in some cases to the pedestals (Fig. 29). Finally, the sideboard in its more modern shape appeared; the pedestals were re-placed by smaller cupboards or drawers, supported on turned or tapered legs

Fig. 29. Adam sideboard, second half of eighteenth century.

(these were six or eight in number), the table continued to hold drawers, and the whole piece was bow- or serpentine-fronted (Pl. 34A). The urns were now dis-carded, and the central bay below the table top was often designed to allow space for a wine cooler, which was made in the same style as the rest of the sideboard. In the Sheraton period some beautiful smaller sideboards were made, often serpen-tine-fronted, and with characteristic turned and reeded legs. As a piece of furniture the sideboard quickly achieved popularity; "the great utility of this piece", wrote Hepplewhite, "has procured it a very general reception." Many were fitted at the back with a brass rail for displaying the family plate.

Early in the nineteenth century the sideboard lost its general lightness and there was a revival of the earlier type of pedestals and table. Urns were not used, but the pedestals were heavier in design than the earlier variety. The cupboards in all types were used for storing the various appurtenances of the dining-room, and sometimes they were lined with metal to keep plates hot, to hold wine bottles, or even to contain water for rinsing. A vivid light on the social habits of the time is thrown by the revelation that they also contained what a foreign visitor, Louis Simond, a Frenchman long domiciled in the United States, delicately described during his visit to England in 1810–11 as "a certain convenient piece of furniture, to be used by anybody who wants it". The reasons for its presence can best be left to Simond's own words: "I once took the liberty to ask why this convenient article

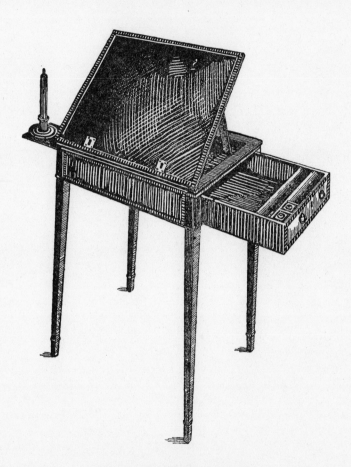

Fig. 30. Sheraton writing table.

was not placed out of the room, in some adjoining closet; and was answered, that, in former times, when good fellowship was more strictly enforced than in these degenerate days, it had been found that men of weak heads or stomachs took advantage of the opportunity to make their escape shamefully, before they were quite drunk; and that it was to guard against such an enormity that this nice expedient had been invented. I have seen the article in question regularly provided in houses where there were no men, that is, no master of the house; the mistress, therefore, must have given the necessary orders to her servants."[1]

Tables. Tables varied so much in size that they are best considered in three categories – small tables, dining-tables and tripod tables. In addition to the side-tables which were components of the early sideboards, the Adam period saw the development of variously shaped small tables – tops, semi-circular when closed, were popular – for tea-drinking, card-playing, writing, dressing, or as pier and con-sole tables. On all the classical ornaments might be carved, inlaid, or painted. These tables usually had either square or turned tapering legs, often fluted, or slender French cabriole legs with knurl or scroll feet. Early in the Adam period the Pembroke table began its long vogue. This type had two flaps (usually semi-circular) and often a drawer (which might be at one end only, with a dummy drawer at the other) (Pl. 34B). The Sheraton period is distinguished for the num-ber of very delicate tables which were made. The high standard of workmanship of the time meant that such tables could be very strong despite their fragile ap-pearance. It was the custom to stand many of these tables about the living rooms of large houses, and as some were expressly designed for ladies' use portability was an important consideration. Among them were little writing tables (Fig. 30) "finished neat, in mahogany or satinwood", work tables with ingenious arrangements of drawers and sliding tops, and nests of tables. From the Pembroke table developed the sofa table, a longer version with small end flaps, standing (unlike the Pem-broke, which almost always had four tapering legs) on a pedestal foot, or on two end supports linked by a stretcher (Pl. 35A). A very typical piece of the Regency period was the round-topped table for writing or for use in libraries. This was mounted either on a turned column resting on curved (and often reeded) legs, or on a solid pedestal base with claw feet. The top had a frieze with drawers, or it might be left open for books.

For dining-tables mahogany remained the favourite wood; its long planks gave both spaciousness and strength. Various forms of the gate-leg were still made. One type consisted of a pair of tables each of which had a fifth leg which could be swung out to support a flap, the whole piece, when fitted up, forming a rectangle. In other examples three units were employed, two semi-circular side tables and a gate-leg table with rectangular flaps; and when a long table was needed for dining, the flaps were raised and the side tables stood at each end. When large single dining-tables were used they did not look cumbersome, despite their size, for they often had tapered and fluted legs on plinth feet (Pl. 35B). Towards the end of the cen-tury some ingenious devices for extending tables were patented, among the best known of which was Gillow's "telescopic" dining-table, with sliders that could be drawn out to hold flaps. About this time there were other distinct changes. It was usual for table tops to be supported on two or more columns each with four legs,

---

[1] L. Simond, *Journal of a Tour & Residence in Great Britain, 1810–11*, 1817.

of the kind known as "pillar and claw". The pillars were turned and the claws, which were at the end of curved and reeded legs, were often in the shape of lion paws and made of brass, with castors. Circular tables, similar to those described above, were also found in the dining-room, mounted on a pillar and claw (Pl. 38A).

Tripod tables were an important element in large houses after 1760, and were used for a variety of purposes, for tea, as occasional tables, and, in slightly modified forms, as candle stands and firescreens. As tea-tables they were in great demand when tea-drinking in public gardens fell into disrepute among fashionable people and was carried on instead in private houses. The tops of these tables were some-times hinged or, in some cases, could be lifted off their supports. In the neo-classic period the solid carved tops, cabriole legs, and ball-and-claw feet were gradually replaced by inlaid tops and modified forms of the cabriole. Later the tripod legs became very delicate and had clearly-defined concave or convex curves resting on dainty, pointed feet (Pl. 38B). In the case of the more elaborate fire-screens and candle stands, the legs were longer and sprang from a small central platform for additional strength.

Bureaux, bookcases, cabinets, etc. Bureaux followed closely the changes in fashion of the chest of drawers with regard to drawer fronts, feet, etc. Fronts and writing flaps, for instance, were often inlaid with classical designs under Adam's influence. Later in the century a curved apron piece often connected the legs be-neath the plinth, and the legs themselves were slender and outward-pointing. About 1800 the writing flap was sometimes replaced by a sliding cylinder or tam-bour front. This treatment was favoured by Sheraton, who indeed claimed that he had found bureaux "nearly obsolete in London; at least . . . among fashionable people", but that he had "endeavoured to retrieve their obscurity by adding to them an open bookcase and modernizing the lower part". Some of these later bureaux were made with slender legs and a single drawer under the writing section.

Where the bureau had a bookcase the latter often had a clear architectural character, as had larger bookcases, cabinets, and similar pieces. The tops were frequently decorated with a broken pediment – angular, swan-neck or curved – though this was by no means universal, for many cabinet-makers preferred a simple straight cornice. Glazing bars of mahogany were extensively used in the second half of the century, and some very graceful patterns were obtainable. In the Adam period cabinets were veneered with woods of contrasting colours (Pl. 38C). Larger pieces of this kind often had a break front, i.e. the central part was made to jut out a little. Shortly after 1800 the traditional design of the bookcase was modified; it was made to a low height so as to leave the walls above free for pictures (Pl. 33B).

Mirrors. There were considerable changes in the design of mirrors after 1760. In the middle of the century large mirrors, particularly the pier glasses which stood between windows, were perhaps the best examples of the rococo and Chinese styles in their most intricate and asymmetrical forms. The classical revival swept these excesses away. Large glasses now usually had rectangular frames which were carved and gilt with decorations of paterae, honeysuckle and festoons surmounted by an urn, bird, etc. (Pl. 36A). Sometimes the more delicate decoration was carried out by mounting a specially prepared composition on metal threads.

Smaller mirrors were oval and rectangular and had narrow frames with surrounds and crests of open work. Carving on frames, however, was soon to be largely replaced by painted decoration.

At the end of the century came another notable change – the general introduction of convex, circular mirrors which had been used in France since the 1750's (and had indeed been illustrated in Ince and Mayhew's *Universal System*). Their frames, moulded and gilt, had a black (ebonized) fillet on the inside edge near the glass, and a reeded outer edge; the hollows of the moulding contained gilt balls. The favourite cresting above the frame was an eagle on a plinth with acanthus (Fig. 31).

Dressing or toilet mirrors – little mirrors on stands fitted with drawers – provided delightful examples of fine craftsmanship. The frames, of rectangular, oval or shield shapes (Fig. 32) swung on two uprights fitted into the stand, which was often bow- or serpentine-

Fig. 31. Circular mirror, about 1800. *Victoria and Albert Museum.*

fronted. Taller dressing glasses, known as cheval or, in Sheraton's words, "horse dressing glasses", stood, as their name implies, on four legs. The uprights followed the prevailing modes of carving, turning or painting, and feet were reeded and curved outwards (Pl. 36B).

Long-case clocks. Though Sheraton described long-case clocks as almost

obsolete in his day in London, they were still being made in the late eighteenth
century, many of them with walnut veneers when this wood had become unfashionable. After 1760, however, mahogany was increasingly used, and the general
tendency was to make the cases broader, the bodies shorter, and the bases heavier,
and thus the slender proportions of the earlier japanned and walnut pieces tended
to disappear. At first dark mahogany was in vogue, with carving and fretwork, but
from about 1770 the emphasis was on finely-figured wood which was often
veneered on a carcase of oak, with inlaid or painted classical designs. Small
classical columns were also found at the sides of the head, and fluted and reeded
pilasters at the front corners of the body. The hood was often surmounted by a
broken finial (Fig. 33). At the very end of the century there was a distinct break

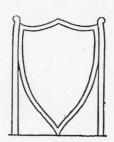

Fig. 32. Toilet mirror,
shield shape.

Fig. 33. Clock hood,
about 1780. *Victoria
and Albert Museum.*

with the traditional design, for some fine pieces had pedestal-shaped bodies,
veneered with mahogany or satinwood and inlaid with various woods, and a
plainer circular dial in a narrow frame, instead of a hood. An important feature
of the period was the great improvement in provincial clock-making. Provincial
clocks tended to be even broader than London ones, and many were made of oak.

Other furniture: country. Little enough is known about the furniture in cottages and smaller farmhouses in remoter areas of the country. In many cottages
the contents must have been extremely primitive, like those seen in Devon by
Louis Simond in 1810–11: "the floors appear to be a pavement of round stones like
the street, – a few seats, in the form of short benches, – a table or two, – a spinning
wheel, – a few shelves." But that cottage furniture of even a simple kind was regarded as a valuable possession is clear from the way it was put to as many uses as
possible, and also handed down in the family for generations. Goldsmith, in his

poem *The Deserted Village*, 1770, wrote of the cottage chest which "contrived a double debt to pay, a bed by night, a chest of drawers by day". In the later eighteenth century furniture could be found in rural districts which dated back to early Stuart and Tudor times. In 1761, for example, Horace Walpole wrote: "Dicky Bateman has picked up a whole cloister full of old chairs in Herefordshire – he bought them one by one, here and there in farmhouses for three and sixpence and a crown apiece. They are of wood, the seats triangular, the backs, arms and legs loaded with turnery. A thousand to one but there are plenty up and down Cheshire too." Such chairs, collected by Georgian devotees of "gothic" furniture, were of a medieval pattern which rural craftsmen had continued to make well into the seventeenth century. It is clear, too, that much of the furniture in country places was made at home. This was true not only of the very poor, but also of people of more substantial station, even of the smaller gentry. At Townend, near Troutbeck, Westmorland, which for several centuries was the home of a well-to-do yeoman family, the furniture (now under the care of the National Trust) was largely the work of many generations of the family, down to the death of the last of the male line in 1914. It could also happen that some cottages contained furniture of distinctly good quality which was passed on to them from the local manor house where it had been discarded in favour of more fashionable pieces – just as the servants' quarters in large houses might have furniture formerly in the best rooms.

Provincial towns. Provincial towns had their reputable cabinet-makers who could supply all classes in the neighbourhood. Some of these craftsmen, indeed, achieved real distinction, like the Gillow family of Lancaster. Even when this firm opened a branch in London about 1760 the furniture was still made at Lancaster for a time and sent to London by sea. From their Lancaster workshop the family supplied furniture to local magnates in that part of the country – such as the Curwens at Workington Hall – where it would obviously be very difficult to get goods from London. In general, however, the upper classes obtained much of their furniture from the capital, whence, as has been seen, cheap furniture could also be supplied to the lower classes by middlemen. In the latter case, the chief consideration was geographical; most of these cheaper goods seem to have been shipped from London as part of the coasting trade. Middle-class people in the provinces usually found local sources of supply sufficient. Parson Woodforde, in his famous diary, describes how he obtained some of the furniture for his parsonage at Weston, some ten miles from Norwich. "Bought this day," he wrote in November, 1789, "of William Hart, Cabinet-Maker on Hog Hill, Norwich, 2 large second hand double-flapped Mohogany Tables, also one second hand Mohogany dressing Table with Drawers, also one new Mohogany Washing-Stand, for all which paid £4.14.6, that is, for the 2 Tables £2.12.6, Dressing Table £1.11.6, Mohogany Wash-stand £0.10.6." Later, in April, 1793, he noted: "About 2 o'clock this Afternoon two Men of Sudbury's at Norwich came with my Side-Board and a large New Mohogany Cellaret bought of Sudbury, brought on the Men's Shoulders all the way and very safe."[1] This last entry is a comment on the state of the country roads at that time.

London. With regard to the furniture used by the lower and lower-middle classes in London, there are only scanty records. A pamphlet of 1767, however, gives the contents of a furnished room rented at half a crown a week by an unmarried clerk in a public office who, with a salary of £50 a year, is described as "in a middling Station". The room has "a half tester bedstead, with brown linsey woolsey furniture, a bed and bolster, half flock, half feathers . . . a small wainscot table, two old chairs with cane bottoms, a small looking-glass six inches by four in a deal frame painted red and black, a red linsey woolsey window curtain".[2] In considering furniture of this sort it is important to remember the cramped living conditions of many Londoners at that time. Lack of cheap transport kept most workers to the immediate vicinity of their places of work. Very many of them lived in furnished rooms as weekly tenants, and even the comparatively small group who reached the superior status of householders normally lived in only part of their houses and let the rest to lodgers. Landlords stocked furnished rooms with much old-fashioned furniture, and those tenants who had to provide their own furniture often bought it by weekly instalments – an old practice which remained popular right through the century. Naturally, better-class tenants could count on improved conditions. C. Moritz, a foreigner who travelled in England in 1782, wrote with appreciation of the room he had rented in London: "I now occupy a large room in front on the ground floor, which has a carpet and matts, and is very neatly furnished; the chairs are covered with leather, and the tables are of mahogany."[3]

This crowded way of life explains the development of what Martin in 1813 called "the fashion of the day, to resort to a number of contrivances for making one piece of furniture serve many purposes". The cabinet-makers' design books, which came out after 1760, had many examples of ingeniously-contrived, space-saving furniture. Some pieces of this kind were patented, such as Eckhardt's portable table and chair (1771), and Gale's bedstead which could close to look like a bookcase or wardrobe (1772). Closely related to the making of this fitted-in furniture was that of invalid furniture, in which some cabinet-makers specialized. In the early nineteenth century, for instance, Pococks of Covent Garden advertised ten different sorts of invalid furniture, including "Patent Sympathetic and Self-Acting Dining Tables, Patent Boethema or Rising Mattresses, Merlin's Reading and Gouty Chairs, and Patent Sofa Beds"[4] (Pl. 31A).

---

[1] *The Diary of a Country Parson* (ed. J. Beresford, 1924–31).

[2] Considerations on the Expediency of Raising . . . the Wages of Servants that are not Domestic, particularly Clerks in Public Offices (B.M.T. 152/4, 1767).

[3] C. Moritz, *Travels in England in 1782* (1924 reprint of trans. of 1795).

[4] This advertisement appears among Foreign Office archives for Spain, 1814 (Pub. Record Office, F.O. 185/50); some of the pieces may have been used by army officers.

REGENCY

THE furniture of any given period is a reflection of what Horace Walpole called "the history of the manners of the age", and this is particularly true of the two decades 1810–30 which saw the important social and economic changes occasioned by the upheaval of the long wars with France (1793–1815) and the increasing tempo of industrialization. The wars had "doubled the cost and trebled the difficulty of genteel living",[1] with the result that the long and salutary domination of good taste in furniture by the upper classes was now drawing to a close. Their place was gradually being taken by the new middle classes, who owed their wealth and position to industry; they lacked the high standards, based on many generations of classical learning, of their predecessors, and they sought fresh styles in the belief that experience and knowledge were no longer necessary to judge decorative forms. Thus the Regency period (which in furniture overlapped the nine years – 1811–20 – when the Prince of Wales was Regent) saw the last phase of the classical development in furniture design which had begun in the seventeenth century. The transition to new forms was made easier through the gradual abandonment of traditional decorative methods like carving and inlay, and through the growing influence of machinery on furniture-making. Wood-working machines, able to carry out almost all the processes which are known today, had been patented by Sir Samuel Bentham between 1791 and 1793, and already in 1807 Thomas Hope in his *Household Furniture* was warning his readers against the debasement of furniture design "through the entire substitution of machinery to manual labour".

It was symptomatic of the changing ideas of the time that much of the formal grace which had distinguished the interiors of great houses in the eighteenth century was disappearing. Louis Simond, visiting Osterley House in 1811, wrote that "Tables, sofas and chairs were studiously *dérangés* about the fire places, and in the middle of the rooms, as if the family had just left them ... Such is the modern fashion of placing furniture, carried to an extreme ... that the apartments of a fashionable house look like an upholsterer's or cabinet-maker's shop."[2]

The best furniture of the period was still, of course, of a high standard in both

---

[1] *The Lady's Keepsake and Maternal Monitor*, 1835.
[2] L. Simond, *Journal of a Tour & Residence in Great Britain 1810–11*, 1817.

design and workmanship, and it should always be related to its setting, which conformed to a carefully thought-out scheme of decoration. But while this is true of the finest pieces, in others the deterioration in standards is all too evident, heralding the decline of the early Victorian era.

The Regency Style. In general terms the Regency style in furniture may be described as a close reproduction or adaptation, carried out in a strong antiquarian spirit, of Græco-Roman types of furniture and forms of decoration. It was inspired by (but was not a close version of) the contemporary French Directoire and Empire styles, and for that reason was for long known as "English Empire". In view of the war period it may seem surprising that English designers should have been influenced by artistic movements in France. This, however, is to look at wars through modern spectacles. France had been too long the arbiter of Europe's taste for war to destroy her prestige, and in any case the connexion of ideas was maintained through the many French craftsmen who took refuge in England from the revolution in their own country. When peace came in 1815 an English writer acknowledged the relationship in these words: "The interchange of feeling between this country and France as it relates to matters of taste, has not been wholly suspended during the long and awful conflicts which have so greatly abridged the intercourse of the two nations, and as usual the taste of both has been improved."[1]

The chief spokesmen for the style in France were Charles Percier and Pierre Fontaine, whose *Recueil de Décorations Intérieures*, 1812, coinciding with Napoleon's widespread conquests, had a great influence throughout Europe. They regarded the study of the decoration of antiquity, with its "simple lines, pure contours and correct forms", as the most fruitful source of inspiration for architects, designers and craftsmen, whose work, they considered, had an essential unity. "Furniture", they wrote, "is too closely allied to interior decoration for the architect to remain indifferent to it. Decoration separated from construction will lead to all sorts of absurdities and misinterpretations." They were at pains, however, to warn against too slavish an imitation of the models of antiquity; these should be "followed, not blindly, but with the discernment allowed by modern manners, customs and materials". Such, then, were to be the principles to be observed: inspiration and admiration tempered with discrimination; the avoidance of mere imitation; the unity of all forms of decoration; and due acknowledgement of modern processes and habits.

In this country the origins of the Regency style in furniture can be clearly seen at the end of the eighteenth century in the work of the talented architect and designer, Henry Holland (1745–1806). With delicacy and a sure touch, he adapted ancient forms into a unified system of decoration without losing the spirit of antiquity or falling into the error of copying contemporary French work. The furniture which he designed for the Prince of Wales at Carlton House (1784) and for Samuel

[1] R. Ackermann, *The Repository of the Arts*, Feb. 1815.

Whitbread at Southill (1795) established his reputation and encouraged imitation. The new style is foreshadowed in Sheraton's *Drawing Book*, 1791–4, and *Cabinet Dictionary*, 1803. But after Holland's death in 1806 the designing of furniture was soon to become an antiquarian pursuit, missing the spirit of antiquity, and seeking to reproduce the actual forms of ancient furniture.

Holland's immediate successor in the field of furniture design was Thomas Hope (1768–1831), whose *Household Furniture and Interior Decoration* was published in 1807. Hope, a man of wide interests and sound scholarship, had been trained as an architect and had travelled extensively throughout the eastern Mediterranean, where he had spent some eight years studying architectural remains. He was a friend of Percier and an admirer of his work. With this background Hope aimed to give the public a range of furniture designs which would "cultivate a new description of art, so urgently wanted and hitherto so rarely possessed". At Deepdene, his house in Surrey, furniture of his own design had been made for the rooms where he kept his collection of antiquities, "forming", he wrote, "the entire assemblage of productions of ancient art and modern handicraft, thus intermixed, into a more harmonious, more consistent and more instructive whole".

These words echoed the sentiments of Percier and Fontaine, but it was too much to expect Hope's and Holland's scholarly approach to be shared or understood by the many craftsmen and designers who now took up the new mode wholeheartedly. Hope was well aware of the dangers of imitation, for he could already see them at work: "extravagant caricatures, such as of late have begun to start up in every corner of the capital, seem calculated for the sole purpose of bringing this new style into disrepute."

The main features of Regency classical furniture were extreme simplicity of outline, large uninterrupted surfaces emphasizing horizontal and vertical lines, subordination of ornament to a minor role, and a stress on solidity – characteristics which Brown summarized in 1820 as "bold in outline, rich and chaste in the ornaments, and durable from the rejection of little parts". The favourite methods of decoration were metal inlay and reeding. At first Greek, Roman and Egyptian antiquities were the models, but as time went on "Grecian severity" became the rule. Interest in Greece was intensified when the Parthenon sculptures were bought by public subscription in 1816, and when the Greeks revolted against the Turks in 1821. Wherever possible, from vase-paintings and similar sources classical Greek furniture was copied, as in the fashionable Grecian sofa and chair; when this could not be done, antique forms were adapted to modern usage. Simple straight lines and bold curves marked this quest for severity. "Grecian" now became a much-favoured word among furniture craftsmen and designers; and in 1836 Loudon's *Encyclopædia* could still describe the "Grecian or modern style" as "by far the most prevalent".[1]

[1] J. C. Loudon, *An Encyclopædia of Cottage, Farm and Villa Architecture and Furniture*, 1836.

The design books. As in the eighteenth century, the current furniture trends were set out in several design books intended for the trade and the general reader. George Smith's *A Collection of Designs for Household Furniture and Interior Decoration* appeared in 1808 and popularized the new style. Smith was a cabinet-maker who described himself as "Upholsterer Extraordinary to His Royal Highness The Prince of Wales", and his book contained 158 plates in colour "studied from the best antique examples of the Egyptian, Greek and Roman styles" with some Gothic and Chinese designs added. Many of the plates showed a somewhat extravagant treatment of the new fashions. In 1820 Richard Brown published *The Rudiments of Drawing Cabinet and Upholstery Furniture*, which had a second and revised edition in 1822. He claimed to be giving craftsmen not only designs for furniture but also the principles which lay behind them (which, he said, the "trivial compositions" of men like Chippendale and Sheraton had omitted to do). His book was a version of the designs of Hope, Percier and Smith, to whom he paid full acknowledgement. In 1826 many coloured designs, with much Greek detail, appeared in *The Practical Cabinet Maker, Upholsterer and Complete Decorator* by Peter and Michael Angelo Nicholson. In the same year George Smith, now styling himself "Upholsterer and Furniture Draughtsman to His Majesty", issued *The Cabinet Maker's and Upholsterer's Guide, Drawing Book and Repository*. He stressed the "perfection of Greek ornament", but included plates of Egyptian, Etruscan, Roman, Gothic and French interiors. He seemed to sense the growing poverty of ideas. About chairs he wrote that "the necessity for economy urged by many at the present day is in itself sufficient to check and weaken the spirit for design, and thus we see nothing but a monotony of character in this article of furniture". Of a different nature from the above books was R. Ackermann's *The Repository of the Arts*, published in monthly parts between 1809 and 1828. Each issue had a section devoted to fashionable furniture illustrated by coloured plates, providing an interesting record of contemporary taste.

Other styles: Gothic. The Regency period was marked by a restless search for new forms. So rapid were the changes in design that we find Thomas Martin in 1820 suggesting "were it practicable, it would be necessary that cabinet, like female fashions, should be published monthly".[1] Smith, in his *Guide* of 1826, confessed that the designs which he had submitted in his *Household Furniture* of 1808 had become wholly obsolete and inapplicable owing to the changes in taste during the last twenty years. It was thus natural that the search for novelty did not stop at Græco-Roman furniture; other styles were attempted, including the gothic, Chinese and Egyptian.

There was, of course, nothing new in the application of gothic motifs to furniture. The "Strawberry Hill" Gothic of Horace Walpole extended its influence long after the rococo period of the mid-eighteenth century which gave it birth.

[1] T. Martin, *The Circle of the Mechanical Arts*, 1820.

The Romantic Revival in literature added to the strong interest in medieval antiquities, with its stress on the picturesque. But both these trends had been aristocratic in origin and remained subordinate to the classical tradition of the upper
classes. Now two new tendencies were at work: one was the growing partiality of
the middle classes, shortly to be the final arbiters of taste, for the Gothic; the other
was the belief that the Gothic was an essentially English style, with a robust vigour
which had a strong emotional appeal. Furniture with gothic motifs, often in the
form of window tracery and pinnacles, was increasingly made for the now fashionable villas and *"cottages ornés"*. In 1836, when Loudon was noting the predomi-
nance of the Grecian style, Sir Samuel Meyrick voiced the opinion that Grecian
forms were no longer suitable for English residences, and that support for the
Gothic was growing.[1]

At this time the Gothic was divided into the Tudor (or Perpendicular) and the
Elizabethan. The former was held to be the improved style introduced by Henry
VII and Henry VIII, and the latter was the English version of the Renaissance.
"Elizabethan" furniture was to have a growing appeal to the popular imagination,
despite criticisms of its spurious character.

Chinese. The revival of the Chinese taste was partly due to the Prince of Wales.
Carlton House, his London residence, had a Chinese drawing-room which is illustrated in Sheraton's *Drawing Book* and for which Henry Holland designed some
furniture in 1790. In 1802 the Prince had a Chinese gallery made at Brighton
Pavilion to show some beautiful Chinese wall-paper which had been presented to
him. But the most important work of this kind at Brighton took place between
1815 and 1821, when extensive improvements were made to the Pavilion under
the direction of John Nash, and the interior was decorated in the Chinese manner,
mainly by Frederick Crace and Robert Jones.[2]

Chinese furniture of this period made free use of dragons, pagodas, mandarins,
and other oriental motifs. Much of it was japanned, especially the cheaper sort
intended for the general public. Another characteristic was the use of imitation
bamboo on chairs and small tables. Like the gothic, the Chinese taste can be considered as part of the cult of the Picturesque; the justification for such styles was
said to lie in the train of romantic and agreeable ideas which they produce (Pls.
39A, 39D, 44, 49).

Egyptian. Unlike the Gothic and Chinese revivals, the Egyptian revival was a
novel development of this period, and one that will always be associated with
Regency furniture. Egyptian antiquities had already been attracting some attention among European artists in the later eighteenth century, and this interest was
considerably quickened in England and France after 1798, the year in which

[1] Sir S. Meyrick, *Specimens of Ancient Furniture*, 1836.
[2] C. Musgrave, *The Royal Pavilion*, 1948.

Napoleon began his Egyptian campaign and in which the French fleet was destroyed by Nelson at the Battle of the Nile. Napoleon took with him a team of French scholars, one of whom, Dominique Vivant Denon, later Director-General of the Museums of France under the First Empire, published in 1802 *Voyage dans la Basse et la Haute Egypte*. This book, with its many illustrations of Egyptian ornament, was soon available in an English translation, and was destined to have an important influence on furniture design. Egyptian motifs were used by Thomas Chippendale the younger in some of the furniture which he made for Sir Richard Colt Hoare at Stourhead, Wiltshire, in 1804–5. The new style was taken up by Thomas Hope, and his *Household Furniture* contains an engraving of the Egyptian decoration and furniture which he had designed for the room containing his collection of Egyptian antiquities at Deepdene. He had many imitators, despite his warnings against indiscriminate use of the style. The vogue was perhaps at its height about 1810, encouraged by the incorporation of Egyptian motifs in Smith's design book of 1808; but it by no means died out rapidly. Ackermann's *Repository* of May 1812, for example, illustrates a library table with supports in the form of sphinxes, although an earlier issue, that of August 1809, had declared that "the barbarous Egyptian style" was already on the wane. Brown's *Rudiments* of 1820 shows examples of decoration with the "Egyptian lotus, or water-lily of the Nile", and similar Egyptian ornament was still being advocated by the Nicholsons and Smith in 1826.

Among the Egyptian motifs found on furniture were the lotus leaf, sphinx heads, lion supports, and, in the more extravagant examples, crocodiles and serpents (Pls. 42B, 43A, 46A). The style could easily get out of hand, especially when it was injudiciously mingled with the gothic and Chinese. The resulting confusion is satirized by Miss Mitford in her account of a visit to Rosedale Cottage:

> Every room is in masquerade: the saloon Chinese, full of jars and mandarins and pagodas; the library Egyptian, all covered with hieroglyphics, and swarming with furniture crocodiles and sphinxes. Only think of a crocodile couch and a sphinx sofa! They sleep in Turkish tents, and dine in a Gothic chapel. . . . The properties are apt to get shifted from one scene to another, and all manner of anomalies are the consequence. The mitred chairs and screens of the chapel, for instance, were mixed up oddly enough with the squat Chinese bronzes, whilst by some strange transposition a pair of nodding mandarins figured amongst the Egyptian monsters.[1]

Woods and decoration. The emphasis on plain lines and unbroken surfaces led to the use of dark and glossy woods, such as mahogany and rosewood, and of woods with boldly striped figure, such as amboyna, calamander and zebra-wood. These gradually replaced the lighter-coloured woods which had been fashionable in the Adam period.

Mahogany remained the established favourite in the library and dining-room. Rosewood, zebra-wood and kingwood all came from Brazil, whence direct trade with Britain had been opened during the Napoleonic Wars. Rosewood, which

[1] M. R. Mitford, *Our Village*, 1824–32.

was also imported from the East Indies, was in great demand; it was a hard, heavy wood marked with dark streaks. Kingwood was finer in the grain than rosewood and generally lighter in tone. Zebra-wood took its name from the streaks of deep brown and white; it could be highly polished and was very fashionable until supplies began to run short after about 1815. Calamander, imported from India, Ceylon and the East Indies, had a hard and fine grain and was of a light brown colour mottled with dark brown and black. Amboyna from the East and West Indies, was distinguished by a figure of small knots and curls, resembling bird's-eye maple, on a warm brown ground. It was the practice of the time to obtain some of these fashionable colours and figures by staining other woods, and this was done even in the case of good furniture. Rosewood, for instance, could be closely simulated by staining wood with logwood and marking the streaks with vitriol. Much furniture was also japanned to accord with the Chinese taste.

At the end of the war with France, French polish was introduced into this country and quickly became popular. It was described by Loudon as by far the best polish "for bringing out the beauties of the wood and giving it a brightness and richness of colour which nothing else hitherto invented can produce". Much old furniture was stripped and the polish, consisting of shellac dissolved in spirit, was then applied. The grain had first to be filled and the substances used for this purpose have subsequently bleached, thus spoiling the furniture.

Both the economic effects of the war period and the changes in taste caused the gradual abandonment of the two decorative processes of inlaying and carving which had been used in the late eighteenth century. The former was found to be too expensive and the latter was fast becoming a decaying craft. According to Martin in *The Circle of the Mechanical Arts*, 1820, only eleven master carvers were then at work in London, and though the old title of "Carvers and Gilders" appeared over the doors of many shopkeepers, it could be "proved that hundreds of the latter never saw a carving tool in their lives". In 1835 the architect, C. R. Cockerell, asserted that a very great dearth of carvers had existed for fifty years.[1]

The principal new decorative medium was brass, which was both cheaper and more durable than the former methods, and also showed up handsomely against dark woods. It was used in a variety of ways on almost all types of furniture: inlays of delicate lines or of more ornamental scrolls and floral and classical motifs; galleries on the tops of sideboards and similar pieces; colonnettes to support galleries and shelves; ornamental beading; wire trellis in the doors or sides of cabinets, bookcases, cupboards, etc.; lion feet on tables; castors on chairs and tables; and ringed, lion mask handles on drawers (Pls. 40A, 41B, 42B, 43B, 46A, 47A and B). Brass inlay was a specialized craft centred in London in the area of St Martin's Lane, and good work of this character found on furniture of the period is a sure indication of its London origin. Chased ormolu work, on the other hand, was a French speciality, and when it is found on English furniture it is most likely

---

[1] Examination of C. R. Cockerell before the Select Committee on Arts and Manufactures, 1835–6.

G

that it was done by immigrant craftsmen. A certain amount of the furniture of this time was also decorated with boulle work – inlay of metal and tortoiseshell – at the "Buhl factory" established by the Frenchman, Louis le Gaigneur, in the Edgware Road about 1815, and at other workshops where English craftsmen carried out this traditional French decoration (Plate 48).

At its best, metal ornament was used in a restrained and delicate fashion, but there was inevitably a tendency to extravagance. In 1820 Brown warned cabinetmakers that a very important part of their skill lay in "harmonizing metals with woods, so as not to overload the articles with buhl, bronze or ormolu, which is too frequently to be seen".

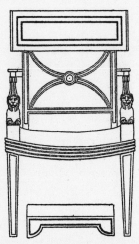

Fig. 34. Armchair from Hope's *Household Furniture*, 1807.

Fashionable furniture: chairs and other seat furniture. There was so much variety in chair design during this period that Brown declared that it baffled "the most skilful artist to produce any new forms". Typical of Hope's influence was the fashionable Grecian chair, which figures prominently in the interior scenes of Henry Moses' *Designs of Modern Costume* (1823). On this kind of chair the rear legs and back formed a bold continuous curve, balanced by a forward curve of the front legs. The cresting rail, following the fashion of the beginning of the century, was a wide board set at shoulder height, generally over-running the uprights.

In the case of armchairs, the arms, which usually had supports coming straight up from the front legs, often swept upwards to join the back uprights near the top, though, in some examples favoured by Hope and Smith, the arms were straight and joined the back about half way up (Figs. 34, 35, 36).

By about 1830 something of this form was still preserved in the backs and rear legs; the cresting rail, however, was now to be found slightly curved in shape and resting on the uprights; while a more noticeable change was in the front legs, which were straight and turned, often ornately.

The bergère continued to enjoy favour; the best examples were made of mahogany and had the seat, back and sides of cane-work. Among other decorative features of the chairs of this period were spiral reeding (Pl. 39C), lion feet and lyre-shaped splats, the latter being a revival of a fashionable motif of the later eighteenth century (Pl. 39B). What were termed "fancy" chairs were often made of beech and painted or japanned (Pls. 39A, 39D), or had turned framework to imitate bamboo. Gothic chairs had their backs carved and fretted to represent tracery, and sometimes had small pinnacles on the back uprights.

The sofa or couch was a prominent piece which now became more fashionable than the settee. The Grecian sofa is described in Ackermann's *Repository*, 1811, as "adapted for the library, boudoir or any fashionable apartment". Where the couch form was employed, based on classical models, there was usually a boldly-curved head-piece and a similarly scrolled end, and as the couch was intended for reclining, there was normally a short arm-rest on one side of the larger end. The legs were of various shapes: lion feet, or outward curving, or turned in the form of tops. Other kinds of sofas had upholstered backs, curved end-pieces of the same

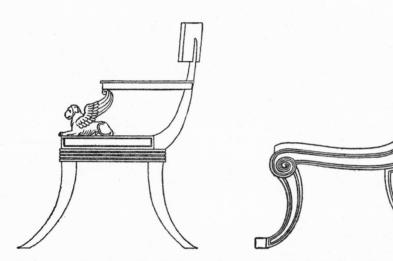

Fig. 35. Armchair from Hope's *Household Furniture*, 1807.

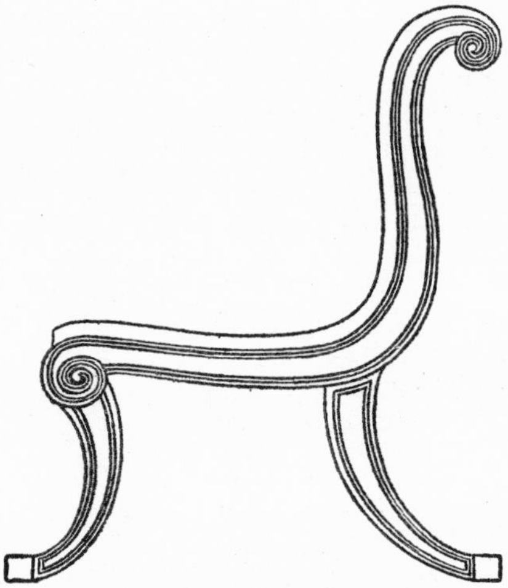

Fig. 36. Chair from Hope's *Household Furniture*, 1807.

height, and usually short feet which curved outwards (Pl. 45). Ottomans (or "Turkey sofas") were also in fashion. They had no backs or sides and were chiefly intended, according to Brown, "for music rooms and picture galleries", though he presented some modified designs for boudoirs and cabinets. The circular ottoman, on which the sitters were back to back, was a novelty, and was used in rooms which had bow windows or circular ends.

Stools were a familiar part of Regency interiors, for window recesses, or to accompany elegant sets of chairs. The X-shape cross frame was in vogue, often with lion feet.

Tables. It was customary in the larger houses to have large dining-tables made up of sections which could be fastened together as required, and several varieties of these were to be found (Pls. 41A, 42A). In the later eighteenth century what was known as a "set of dining-tables" had three units – a centre table with rectangular flaps supported on gate-legs, and two end tables with rectangular or semi-circular tops. After 1800 sectional tables frequently had their supports in the form of pillars and claws, generally, as Sheraton wrote in 1803, "four claws to each pillar, with brass castors". Tables of this kind could be made up to any required length, for the sections, each with pillar and claws, were bolted together with metal clips. For calculating the length of table for a dinner-party, two feet for each diner was the accepted rule. The method of fitting separate tables together had its disadvantages, and a number of patents for single extending tables were taken out, notably by Richard Gillow (1800), Richard Brown (1805), and George Remington (1807). They showed much ingenuity of construction. The description, for example, of Brown's table, which had straight turned legs, states that "the end rails of the table frame are connected by pieces of wood so jointed together as to form what are commonly called lazy-tongs".

Though pillars and claws were so fashionable, they seem to have caused a certain amount of inconvenience. *The Repository* in 1810 illustrates a patent sideboard and dining-table (given the name "Trafalgar" because one was supplied, it is claimed, to Nelson) in which the table could be pushed into the sideboard and extra flaps kept in the drawers; the advantage being that the "feet of this table are completely out of the way ... in this particular they far excel the claw tables". It

was for this same reason that Smith in 1808 recommended the use of the circular dining-table supported on a pedestal or circular base, and this type came into wide use, especially as it had the additional advantage of avoiding invidious distinctions among guests when seated at dinner.

The sofa table was also in general demand after 1800. The table-top, when its two small end-flaps were extended, was some five to six feet long, and about two feet wide, and it was supported either by two end supports linked by a stretcher, or by a pedestal on a small platform with splayed feet (Pl. 40A). This attractive and useful table was often fitted with two drawers in the frieze and was intended for the library, drawing-room, boudoir or any ladies' apartment, for reading, writing or drawing. It was a development of the smaller Pembroke table, which it

Fig. 37. Work-table, from Ackermann's *Repository*, 1811.

did not, however, supersede, for the latter was still fashionable and now often had, like the sofa table, rectangular end flaps with rounded corners.

Small tables of all kinds were placed about the living-rooms. Sometimes nests of tables were found, especially little sets of four, known as "quartetto" tables. Ladies' work-tables were in constant use, and many varieties of these were made by the cabinet-makers in their search for novel designs. A pouch for needlework was a usual feature, together with a lifting top over a small compartment or set of drawers (Fig. 37). Combined work-and-games tables were also popular; an example made by Morgan and Saunders in 1811 and illustrated in *The Repository* was in the fashionable "Brazil wood" (i.e. zebra-wood), and was fitted for "seven different accommodations", including reading, writing, needlework, chess and backgammon. Tables of this kind, and other sorts of combined games-and-card tables, tended to oust the old-established card-tables, for fewer of these were now made; one does find, however, "loo tables" specially made for the popular card game of the period.

In libraries the pedestal table with knee-hole and flanking drawers or cupboards followed the traditional form (Pl. 40B), except for the addition of details like lion feet and Egyptian figures to accord with changing fashions. A more novel type was the Carlton House writing-table, which made its appearance at the end of the eighteenth century. This had a superstructure of small cupboards and drawers running round the back and sides of the top, and drawers in the frieze. The reason for its name is a mystery, as there is no evidence to connect it with Carlton House.

Side or pier tables continued in use in dining-rooms, often supported by lion monopodia or Egyptian figures. Some examples had a low platform at the base and were occasionally fitted with silvered glass on the inside and back, "to produce", in Smith's words (1826), "a reflecting effect from the china objects which are usually placed in such situations". The tops of some of these tables were of solid marble (Pls. 43A, 46A, 47A).

Bookcases. For larger libraries cabinet-makers continued to make the traditional type of bookcase in two stages, in which the lower stage of cupboards was surmounted by rows of shelves enclosed by glazed doors. Classical proportions were maintained, with some concessions to prevailing decorative changes. Thomas Hope, for instance, designed a bookcase of this kind for Deepdene which had carved sphinx heads on the pilasters separating the four glass doors, and four lion monopodia on the lower stage.

A distinctly new piece in fashion in the early nineteenth century was the dwarf bookcase, the doors of which were either glazed or fitted with a trellis of brass wire. It was made purposely low to leave "an ample space on the wall above for the placing of pictures" (Smith, 1826). Several varieties were found, in use in the sitting-room and boudoir as well as in the library. One type shown by Brown in 1820 was a lady's bookcase with cabinet, the object of the latter being "to contain ladies' jewels, ancient medals and precious stones, with other valuable curiosities" – an interesting reminder that the hobby of collecting curios, which had stimulated the production of cabinets in the late seventeenth century, was still very much alive among richer people.

The revolving circular bookcase was an innovation of this period. One kind was patented by Benjamin Crosby in 1808 and was described as "a machine or stand for books, which may be made either circular, square or any other convenient shape, and which may be turned or moved at pleasure, with cases to receive books, as well as various other articles and things". This type and others of the same kind followed the general principles of a central shaft to which cylinders holding the shelves were screwed.

The trend towards lightness in bookcases produced one of the most attractive of the smaller Regency pieces, the little set of portable open shelves which could be

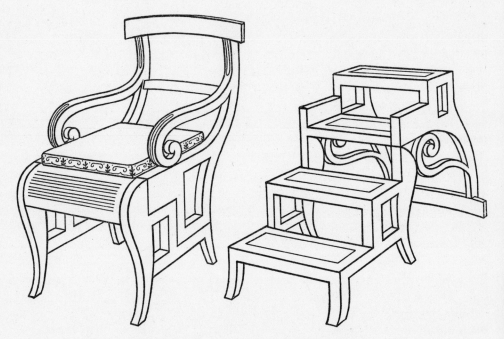

Figs. 38 and 39. Combined library chair and steps, from Ackermann's *Repository*, 1811.

carried by ladies about the room, or from one room to another. The sides of the shelves were often made of brass wire. There were many other kinds of small bookcases (Pl. 47B).

In large libraries, for reaching the books on the upper shelves, library steps were indispensable, and some of these were in the form of folding steps ingeniously fitted into chairs, stools and tables; the back of a library chair, for example, could be swung over to the ground, disclosing a small set of steps (Figs. 38, 39).

Sideboards and other dining-room furniture. In the early years of the nineteenth century the lighter kind of sideboard associated with Hepplewhite and

Sheraton went out of favour, and there was a revival of the sideboard table fitted with pedestal cupboards which had been developed from the designs of Robert Adam. This was the type favoured by Smith in 1808. It soon became a commodious piece of furniture and lost its former graceful proportions. The pedestal cupboards, which often tapered slightly almost to floor level, were used as cellarets and plate-warmers, and on them often stood knife-boxes of similar tapering shape, in place of the urns which had been found in the Adam period. All these fittings were necessary, as the servants still washed the glasses and cutlery in the dining-room between courses. A characteristic feature of the later sideboards of this type was the high back-piece rising above the table-top (Fig. 40).

Sideboard tables, without the pedestal cupboards, were also in use. These tables were large, and sometimes had animal supports which stood on a plinth. A cellaret or wine-cooler, commonly of sarcophagus form at this time, stood in a central position beneath the table, and drawers with brass lion-mask handles were often found in the frieze. An elaborate brass gallery usually ran along the back of the table.

Several other accessories were necessary in the fashionable dining-room. Dumb waiters continued in use, but with rectangular tiers and supports of pillars and claws instead of the circular tiers and tripod bases of the earlier varieties. One of the two pieces called a "Canterbury" (the other was a music-stand) was a plate-and-cutlery stand described by Sheraton as "a supper tray, made to stand by a table at supper, with a circular end and three partitions cross wise, to hold knives, forks and plates at that end, which is made circular on purpose."

Chiffoniers, chests of drawers, etc. The French-inspired commode of the later eighteenth century, with its curved surfaces and decoration of fine inlay and painting, did not lend itself to the bold outlines which were now in favour, and its place was taken by the chiffonier. This was not a new name, for it had been in use in Chippendale's time, but the chiffonier of the eighteenth century seems to have been modelled on the French chiffonière, which was a small case of drawers on legs, whereas the Regency chiffonier was a low open cupboard with shelves for books (Pl. 47A). It held the books which were in constant use, and was found in both the drawing-room and the library. Sometimes a small set of shelves stood on the top.

The chest of drawers retained its traditional form, and continued to be straight- or bow-fronted. Since the end of the eighteenth century, however, new features were spirally reeded columns at the front corners (about 1810 spiral reeding began to replace the plainer vertical reeding), and a deep frieze above the top drawer. Also characteristic of the period were lion-mask handles. The old-established tall-boy or chest-on-chest was only occasionally made at this period, owing to the inconvenient height of the upper drawers.

Other small pieces. Among the newer pieces of the period were the what-not, a portable open stand with four uprights enclosing shelves for books and ornaments, and the music Canterbury, a small stand usually mounted on castors, with partitions for music books, and sometimes small drawers for sheets of music (Pl. 46B). The fire- or pole-screen, necessary to give protection from the intense heat of open fires, was not, of course, a novelty, but it now underwent two distinct changes: the former tripod base gave way to a solid base, and the screen took the form of a banner hung from a bar on the upright. The teapoy, a small three- or four-legged table or stand which was not originally associated with tea, was also in use in drawing-rooms at this time (Fig. 41).

Mirrors. Shortly after 1800 the circular convex mirror, made in varying sizes from a foot to perhaps three feet in diameter, became very popular in this country after a vogue of half a century in France. The gilt frame had a hollow moulding for which a filling of evenly-spaced gilt balls was a common form of decoration; the outer edge was usually reeded, with a reeded ebonized fillet on the inner edge next to the glass. This type of mirror, surmounted by a carved eagle with outstretched wings, or by acanthus foliage, and sometimes fitted with candle branches, was a prominent feature of Regency interiors.

In the living-rooms of the wealthier houses large mirrors continued to be fashionable. The chimney-glass, set over the chimney-shelf and extending for most of its length, was in a gilt frame which normally had a pilaster at each end and a straight cornice above. Beneath the cornice a hollow moulding was often found, decorated, like the frame of the circular mirror, with a row of balls. The glass did not always extend over the whole area of the frame, for sometimes there was a deep frieze below the cornice, and this was decorated with classical figures in low relief, or with a painting. Large pier-glasses were also found, extending in some cases up to the ceiling.

Mirrors were deliberately placed to catch the reflections within a room or between rooms. "A pier-glass", wrote Loudon, "placed opposite the chimney glass always has an agreeable effect, as they reflect one another; so that the size of the room is doubled, from whichever end the spectator directs his view." And at night time mirrors gave added attraction to the much-improved illumination provided by the large cut-glass chandeliers suspended from the ceiling. The angularity of the many small pieces of faceted glass in the great lustres was noted by Archibald Alison, whose *Essays on the Nature and Principles of Taste* ran into six editions between 1790 and 1825, in the following words:

In a Lustre, one of the most beautiful productions of this manufacture, all is angular. The Form of the Prism, one of the most regular and angular of all Forms, obtains everywhere, the Festoons even are angular, and instead of any winding or waving Line the whole surface is broken into a thousand little Triangles.

One of the favourite kinds of smaller mirrors was the cheval or horse dressing-glass, a toilet mirror in an upright rectangular frame on four legs. The glass frame pivoted on screws set in the uprights, or could be moved up and down by means of a weight within the frame ("the same as a sash-window": Sheraton).

Other furniture. The search for novelty was reflected in the number of patents which were taken out in this period for furniture, fittings and upholstery. Whereas between 1620 and 1799 thirty-three patents altogether were registered under these headings, no less than sixty-eight were taken out between 1800 and 1830, fifty-three during the years 1810–30.[1] They included invalid furniture, extending

Fig. 40. Sideboard c. 1810–15, with wine-cooler

tables (to which reference has been made) and chairs, adjustable screens and bed-frames, and several kinds of castors. These last were an indication of the growing massiveness of furniture.

It was at this time that High Wycombe in Buckinghamshire became an important manufacturing centre of Windsor chairs. For at least a century previously these chairs had been made in the woods around the town. "Bodgers" turned the legs, stretchers and sticks on their pole lathes; benchmen made the seats, bows and splats; and framers saw to the assembling and finishing. Local woods were used, mainly elm for the "dished" seats, ash, yew and willow for the bows, and beech and ash for the legs and sticks. In 1805, according to local tradition, Samuel Treacher, a farmer, started chair-making as a winter occupation for his hands on Marlow Hill. Thomas Widginton came to High Wycombe to teach these men how

[1] Patent Office, Old Series of Abridgements of Specifications relating to Furniture and Upholstery 1620–1866, 1869.

to assemble the chairs from parts supplied by the rural craftsmen, and about 1810 he set up the first furniture factory in the town. It is known that by 1837 Widginton was a substantial property-owner with his own Chair Manufactory.[1] Windsor chair-making was not, of course, confined to High Wycombe or to Buckinghamshire; it was an old rural craft which continued in other parts of the country. In fact, Loudon referred to Windsors as "one of the best kitchen chairs in general use in the midland counties of England".

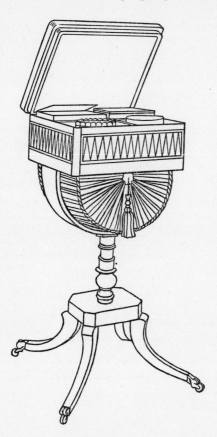

Fig. 41.   Teapoy, rosewood with parquetry decoration, *c. 1820 Victoria and Albert Museum.*

Other cottage furniture varied considerably both in quantity and quality. In poor homes in out-of-the-way areas such as Devonshire and Cornwall only the most rudimentary kind might be found. But more comfortable furniture could be seen in those places where it could be supplied cheaply from London (perhaps by sea) or from other convenient sources of supply; or else the cottage might occasionally have pieces from the local manor house which had got rid of them to make was for a re-furnishing.

Where the farmhouse had profited from the rising food prices of the war period the opportunity was often taken to replace the old furniture with something more up-to-date. This excited the indignation of William Cobbett, who regarded the change as aping one's betters. He described a Surrey farmhouse in 1825 in these terms:

Everything about this farmhouse was formerly the scene of plain manners and plentiful living. Oak clothes-chests, oak bedsteads, oak tables to eat on, long, strong and well supplied with joint stools. . . . One end of this once plain and substantial house had been moulded into a 'parlour': and there was a mahogany table, and the fine chairs, and the fine glass, and all as bare-faced upstart as any stock-jobber in the kingdom can boast of.[2]

It was an interior of this kind which Gillray showed in his etching of 1809, "Farmer Giles and his wife showing off their daughter Betty to their Neighbours" (shown as Plate 27 in Trevelyan's *Illustrated English Social History*).

[1] F. Roe, *Windsor Chairs*, 1953.   [2] W. Cobbett, *Rural Rides*, 1821–32.

EARLY VICTORIAN

THE thirty years from 1830 to 1860 are the most neglected in the whole history of English furniture. There is hardly a book or even an article devoted to early Victorian furniture, and no systematic public or private collections of it. Those few students who venture beyond 1830 usually leap straight on to William Morris and the 1860's, with nothing more than a cursory glance at the Great Exhibition of 1851 to cover the intervening years. Indeed, the total neglect of the period is best epitomized by the fact that of the ten names listed by Matthew Digby Wyatt in 1856 (*Report on the Furniture at the Paris Exhibition of 1855*) as representing the most prominent furniture designers during the previous thirty years, only one – A. W. N. Pugin – is now remembered; three – Bridgens, Whitaker and Dwyer – though entirely forgotten, can still be identified because they published surviving pattern-books, while the remaining six have sunk into total oblivion.

During all other periods since 1700, furniture design has owed much to the inspiration of architects. During the early Victorian period this was not so. With the exception of Pugin, the only architects who seem to have designed furniture were Philip Hardwick and C. J. Richardson. Moreover, even the leading general designers did little in the field of furniture. The two best – Alfred Stevens and Owen Jones – turned to furniture design only at the end of their careers, after 1860, and we have to drop down to secondary figures such as W. B. Scott, L. N. Cottingham and J. K. Collings, before we find any consistent furniture designing.

Documentary evidence. In face of these difficulties, any serious study of the subject must start from an analysis of the surviving *documentary* evidence, and not from an inspection of the increasing quantities of so-called early Victorian furniture now being handled by furniture dealers. This surviving furniture is often quite atypical, and a survey based on it would only perpetuate that process of selective survival which over-emphasizes what is quaint but freakish, at the expense of what is dull but typical.

The available documentary evidence can be listed under seven heads. First, and most valuable of all, are the working records of the leading manufacturers. Unfortunately only one such series – the copious records of Messrs Gillow of

Lancaster – appears to have survived intact. In view of the fact that, of all the great early Victorian cabinet-making firms, only two others – Messrs Trollope and Messrs Holland – still survive, and that both have lost all their earlier records, it seems doubtful whether others will come to light. Certainly there can now be little hope of discovering those of long-defunct firms such as Arrowsmith, Banting, Dalziel, Dowbiggin or Wilkinson, whose work was most typical of the period.

Second in importance are illustrated trade catalogues. Very few have so far been traced, and most relate to the single firm of William Smee of Finsbury Pavement. Although their plates are especially valuable as providing irrefutable testimony to actual production, they are almost always undated, and must, therefore, be used with great circumspection.

Third are the cheaper pattern-books with lithographed plates and no text, put together with no pretence of originality by hack designers for the use of firms too small or unenterprising to employ their own designer. They provide a record of the average taste of the times. They are best represented by the many volumes put out by Thomas King for the 1830's, and by Henry Wood for the 1840's and Henry Lawford for the 1850's. Requiring a different interpretation is the fourth category, namely the more expensive volumes, usually with engraved plates and some text, put out by designers with some claim to creative ability – such as Bridgens, Whitaker or Peter Thomson – and consequently including a high proportion of more fanciful "prestige" designs. Although many of these designs were probably never executed, and although they cannot, therefore, be taken as a safe guide to general production, they are often useful as illustrating the beginnings of stylistic changes which only later became fashionable.

A fifth source of information is existing furniture which can be dated and attributed by the evidence of surviving accounts or similar records. Further research would no doubt disclose much more of this than the few examples investigated and illustrated for this article. It is, perhaps, unfortunate that for obvious reasons, some of the most readily available evidence of this kind is provided by furniture associated with the Royal family – as, for example, the library-furniture commissioned for Windsor by William IV, the furniture at Kensington Palace, the furniture designed by Henry Whitaker for Osborne, or the furniture in bedrooms occupied by Queen Victoria during visits to places such as Woburn Abbey or Stoneleigh Abbey. Such furniture is liable to give a distorted picture if used as an index to the dating of stylistic changes, for throughout the early Victorian period (and indeed from the death of George IV onwards) the taste of the Court tended to be some ten years or so behind that of London society generally; apart also from the atypical influence of Prince Albert's German associations.

The sixth category consists of the records of furniture designs registered for copyright purposes with the Patent Office from 1839 onwards. These are meagre for every category except papier-mâché and cast-iron. The last category consists of the copious records and illustrations, both official and unofficial, of the furniture displayed at the various exhibitions of the period, namely at Manchester in 1846, the four Society of Arts exhibitions in London from 1847 to 1850, Birmingham 1849, the Crystal Palace 1851, Dublin and New York 1853, and Paris 1855.

Exhibition furniture. These records have been deliberately placed last because they give an entirely misleading picture of the average production of the times. The illustrated catalogue of the Great Exhibition of 1851, being far more readily accessible than any of the other documentary sources just listed, has too often been used as exclusive evidence of early Victorian taste, without allowance for the fact that the furniture displayed in the Crystal Palace – in common with all the other exhibits – was mainly shown for its novelty and inventiveness. Richard Redgrave, R.A., was certainly not exaggerating when he criticized the whole principle of international exhibitions, and wrote that: "Each manufacturer is striving his utmost to attain notice and reward … by an endeavour to catch the consumers by startling novelty or meretricious decoration, leading, in most cases, to an extreme redundancy of ornament. The goods are like the gilded cakes in the booths of our country fairs, no longer for use, but to attract customers." (*Report on the Present State of Design as Applied to Manufactures*, 1857.)

Where – as with Gillows' – it is possible to compare their exhibits with their everyday production, it is clear that the former were in no way typical of the latter, and the same was, no doubt, equally true of the other leading firms such as Jackson and Graham, Johnstone and Jeanes, and Snell. Moreover, the exhibition catalogues (especially the illustrations, which were paid for by the exhibitors) give a false impression of the relative importance of the various manufacturers, and in particular greatly exaggerate the real weight of the West End luxury firms such as Morant, John Webb, Levien, and Toms and Luscombe, who staged elaborate special displays of their wares. Indeed, so distorting are the conclusions usually drawn from these exhibitions, that it is advisable to dismiss the two principal ones before passing to a positive analysis of early Victorian styles.

The first misconception is that early Victorian furniture is fussy and elaborate, and generally covered with carving. This was certainly true of almost all the Crystal Palace exhibits. Few were quite so preposterous as the much-publicized bog-oak examples of Arthur J. Jones and Co. of Dublin, with carving so elaborate that a description of its symbolic significance required several pages, but even respectable firms such as Howard and Sons, and George Trollope and Sons, placed their main emphasis on pieces "enriched by carved floriated ornament of cunning workmanship", to quote a contemporary account. The same pre-occupation is shown by the way in which leading firms such as Snell and Co. and the Coalbrookdale Iron Company, when they wished to improve their standing by some specially-commissioned prestige pieces, turned for designs not to leading architects, as would have been normal in other periods, but to popular sculptors such as Baron Marochetti and John Bell.

This emphasis on decorative carving was, no doubt, the inevitable result of the competitive ostentation fostered by the spirit of the Exhibition, but it can also be partly explained by the influence of the propaganda and prizes of the Society of Arts in their preparations for the Exhibition, in which the personal enthusiasm of Prince Albert – with his memories of German peasant wood-carving – was a strong ingredient. It cannot, however, be said to have had any influence on the general run of furniture production. Indeed, its only noticeable effect, outside the Exhibition, was to encourage skilful wood-carvers such as W. G. Rogers – often referred to by contemporary commentators as the "Victorian Grinling Gibbons" – and Thomas Wallis of Louth, and to stimulate noble patronage for the curious school of Warwick wood-carving represented by the firms of William Cookes and James Morris Willcox. Both these firms, and later the firm of William Kendall, who had originally been apprenticed to Willcox, produced between 1848 and 1860 a considerable quantity of carved furniture in a highly elaborate "naturalistic" style, in which every article was enriched with carving with a narrative or symbolic significance, executed with the attention to detail of a *trompe l'œil* (Pls. 61–64). Their work is seen at its worst in such over-carved monstrosities as the "Kenilworth Buffet" (1851) now at Warwick Castle, and at its best in Cookes's Alscot Park buffet (designed by Hugues Protat for the Great Exhibition of 1851 but actually shown at the Manchester Art Treasures Exhibition, 1857, Pl. 61), or Willcox's splendid sideboard (1858) now at Charlecote Park (Pl. 64).

Early Victorian conservatism. The second misconception for which the Great Exhibition catalogues have been mainly responsible is that early Victorian furniture was subject to a constantly shifting succession of stylistic revivals in which it is impossible to discern any consistent thread. A close examination of contemporary pattern-books – and particularly of the Gillow records – shows, on the contrary, that furniture fashions changed remarkably little between 1835 and 1860, and that the Early Victorian period was in this respect far more conservative than either the Regency or the mid-Victorian. One of the clearest testimonies to this conservatism is the fact that Thomas King's pattern-book *The Modern Style of Cabinet Work Exemplified*, 1829, was reissued without alteration in 1862, while the furniture sections of J. C. Loudon's compendious *Encyclopædia of Cottage, Farm, and Villa Architecture*, 1833, were incorporated with nothing omitted and very little added in all the later editions (1842, 1846, 1857). By comparison it would be quite impossible to imagine a pattern-book of 1810 being issued unchanged in 1840, or one of 1850 being reissued in 1880.

This Early Victorian conservatism may well have been the direct result of that rise of the *nouveau riche* patron, which is usually held to have upset all traditional standards of taste. Their lack of independent æsthetic standards, and their conformist social aspirations, would seem as likely to have counselled a prudent acceptance of established conventions as to have led these new patrons into any stylistic adventures. Moreover, this tendency would have been reinforced by the fact that, as the demand for furniture increased, so did the proportion that was produced by firms without their own designers, and which were, therefore, compelled to keep to the repetition of stock patterns with no pretence of originality – a trend which was strengthened by the detailed price-schedules set out in successive editions of the *London Cabinet-Makers' Union Book of Rules*, 1811, 1824, 1836, which gave the small employer every incentive to keep to the accepted patterns, rather than to launch out on new designs and thus risk pricing troubles with his workmen.

Before passing to an analysis of the consistent style which subsisted throughout most of the Early Victorian period, we must first glance at the very rapid and radical stylistic changes which were its prelude, over the years 1827 to 1835. Fortunately their documentation is made relatively easy by the survival of a wide variety of pattern-books covering these crucial years. The key to the changes was, of course, the breakdown of that long hegemony of the various styles based on the antique – whether Greek, Roman, Pompeian or Egyptian – which until 1827 had been challenged only by the Gothic – and then in only a very limited field. By 1830, however, they were faced with two new competitors – the revived Louis XIV style, and the revived Elizabethan.

The "Louis XIV" revival. The reintroduction of Louis XIV furniture and furnishings can be dated precisely to 1827, when Crockford's new club-house was decorated by Philip and Benjamin Dean Wyatt. This was interpreted by the London decorators as authority to abandon the austerities of the "Modern Grecian", and to revert to the opulent splendours of the *ancien régime*, whether in their baroque or rococo forms. Already by 1828 the change is visible in patterns for mirrors, frames, window cornices and the like, with scrolls and shells replacing the hitherto ubiquitous anthemion. By 1830 it had spread to movable furniture, and particularly to drawing-room chair-backs. Although evidently welcomed by the trade, this change was unanimously condemned by architects and designers who saw it as opening the gates to any hack furniture-maker who could now throw together an assortment of botched-up scrolls, cover them with gilding, and label them "in the old French style".

A critical attitude to the new style had already been voiced by George Smith (*Cabinet-Maker's and Upholsterer's Guide, Drawing-Book and Repository*) immediately after the opening of Crockford's Club, with the comment that "As this mansion is solely appropriated to nightly purposes of pleasure, perhaps such a taste may be in unison with the wasteful transfer of property made in such establishments." Similar views were presented before the Select Committee on Arts and Manufactures (1835), by witnesses such as J. B. Papworth and C. R. Cockerell, who not only deplored the licence provided to inferior designers by the new style, but also pointed out how what had started as a revival of the baroque splendours of Louis XIV very rapidly degenerated by its own internal momentum into indiscriminate borrowing from the rococo trivialities of Louis XV. Despite this almost universal condemnation by serious architects, however, the spread of these "old French" styles was very rapid, especially for drawing-rooms and boudoirs. The extent to which the change was limited to these more feminine rooms, while leaving the furnishings of more masculine quarters relatively untouched, is very clearly shown by the suites of furniture supplied in 1833-4 by Messrs W. and C. Wilkinson to Goldsmiths' Hall, under the supervision of the architect, Philip Hardwick (Pls. 51, 52A, 53A, 58. It will be seen that, whereas the furniture for the Court Drawing-Room is entirely in the new style, that for the Court Dining-Room and for the Court Room itself shows little variation from the standard patterns of the 1820's. Indeed, for the more traditionalist institutions, these "Modern Greek" designs remained in vogue for at least ten years longer, as witness the furniture designed by Henry Whitaker for the Conservative Club in 1844 (Pls. 53A, 54).

The "Elizabethan" revival. The Elizabethan revival was, by contrast, a conscious creation of the more sophisticated architects and designers such as C. J. Richardson. It first appears in furniture pattern-books just after 1830, directly inspired, no doubt, by the plates in T. F. Hunt's *Exemplars of Tudor Architecture and Furniture*, 1829-30, closely followed by Henry Shaw's *Specimens of Ancient Furniture*, 1832-6. In the early 1830's it was mainly limited to the making up of pseudo-Elizabethan cupboards and coffers out of old fragments, by firms such as Samuel Hanson, and James Nixon (see Loudon's *Encyclopædia* and Georges Fildes' *Elizabethan Furniture*, 1844). After about 1838 it takes its place in all the pattern-books in the form of strap-work carving applied to mirror-frames, sideboard-backs and the like. This Elizabethan revival was supported by the same arguments which were used to condemn the revival of the French styles. It was indisputably British; it was rich without being vulgar; and its coarse vigour did not overtax the somewhat limited finesse of the average British carver. Moreover, its romantic and baronial associations were, of course, entirely in keeping with current literary preoccupations.

By about 1835 both the Louis XIV and the Elizabethan styles had clearly established their right to equal respectability with the Gothic and the "Grecian", and the long hegemony of the latter had finally ended. The change is summed up by the distinction between two of Thomas King's titles: in 1829 he published *The Modern Style of Cabinet Work Exemplified*, whereas in 1834 his *Designs for Carving and Gilding* bore the subtitle *in a variety of styles*. With four quite different styles legitimate, there was now no obstacle to an even more catholic eclecticism, and during the later 1830's we find an astonishing proliferation of titles, including the *Arabesque, the French Renaissance, the Cinquecento*, and so on. Indeed, the most noticeable feature of the pattern-books of the years 1835 to 1850 – best exemplified by Henry Whitaker's *Practical Cabinet-Maker*, 1847 – is the determination that no design should be presented without an attribution to some historic style, and that the greatest possible variety of stylistic titles should be devised for this purpose.

It would be quite wrong, however, to take this eclecticism at its face value for, oddly enough, it was just when it first became all-embracing – around 1835 – that we can first discern the emergence of a consistent and distinguishable Early Victorian style. We may, in fact, claim that it was only when the rigid classical hegemony had been finally broken, and when designers could at last give form to their personal fantasies in a now unfettered eclecticism, that the real spirit of the period begins to achieve spontaneous expression in its furniture. Moreover, so strong was the appeal of historicism at this time that even the most individual inventions had to be designated as in some earlier style, and we should not be surprised, therefore, to find designs which bear the unmistakable Early Victorian stamp, and which could not possibly have been produced at any other time, being solemnly described as "in the purest François Premier taste". One of the fascinations of Early Victorian furniture is the way in which its original quality is often clearest in just those cases where the designer evidently believed himself to have been most faithfully following historical precedent. This is particularly clearly seen in those frequent cases where the same designer has worked in a different style for each room – Gothic for the hall, Elizabethan for the library, Louis XIV for the drawing-room, and so on – but has, nevertheless, left a consistent Early Victorian stamp on each in turn.

Emphasis on comfort. It must be admitted that it is easier to refer to this Early Victorian style in general terms than to list its distinguishing characteristics in detail. They can be more readily illustrated than described. Paradoxically, in an age that was so obsessed with problems of stylistic purity, its keynote was the subordination of all stylistic considerations to the over-riding consideration of comfort. In this it contrasts sharply not only with the 1820's (as witness the primacy of stylistic criteria in the designs of Richard Brown, George Smith and the Nicholsons), but equally with the mid-Victorian period, in which – contrary to general belief – comfort once more took second place to various stylistic mannerisms, whether derived from the Middle Ages, from Sheraton or from Japan. A similar contrast also differentiates this early Victorian style from developments in France, and makes it possible to claim it as the first English style which marked a clear-cut divergence from contemporary French trends. It is perhaps no accident, therefore, that one of the earliest recognitions of its emergence, with a clear analysis of its revolutionary emphasis on comfort, should be found in a French discussion of the difference between French and English furniture as demonstrated by the Paris Exhibition of 1834. (Stéphane Flachat, *L'Industrie: Exposition de 1834*.)

Increased use of upholstery. An obvious corollary to this concentration on comfort was the increased use of padding and upholstery of all kinds, and in

H

particular the evolution for the first time of articles of furniture in which the shape is determined much more by the upholstery than by the framework which it covers. It is sometimes suggested that this development can be related to technical advances in spring construction. In fact, however, these had already been made in the first decade of the century, and a more plausible explanation of these Early Victorian changes was the great improvement in cheap worsted covering-materials resulting from the expansion of Yorkshire power-loom weaving during the 1830's. Although these upholstery changes directly affected only chairs, sofas, ottomans and the like, they influenced, by association, the shapes of all furniture, and it is precisely the rounding-off of all corners and the elimination of all angularities and surface irregularities which are the main distinguishing characteristics of the Early Victorian style. All sharp outlines are smoothed down, rectangular frameworks become oval or semi-circular, edges are bevelled, and projecting pediments or finials are removed. At the same time all crispness or spring disappears from members such as table-supports or chair-backs, and is replaced by a uniform, flabby, unadventurous, heavy-handed curve – a curve which almost gives the wood the appearance of having been squeezed from a tube, and which is contrasted not only with the taut and basically rectilinear outlines of the Regency, but equally with the elegant twistings of the "old French" styles.

Parallel with these developments went a tendency to merge the separate parts of each piece of furniture into a unified, undifferentiated whole. Arms and backs of sofas are joined together in a single enclosing sweep. Front and sides of chiffoniers are likewise embraced in a single enveloping semi-circle. The distinction between pedestal and base in the standard Regency loo-table is obliterated. Moreover, this process was visually accentuated by the virtual elimination of all the many processes by which cabinet-makers have traditionally varied the colour and texture of their surfaces. Inlay, marquetry and boulle-work, and the use of gilding and ormolu, went out of fashion for all normal domestic furniture soon after 1830, and it was not until about 1855 that there was any sign of their revival. The same tendency affected all knobs and handles, which were now usually made of plain wood rather than of metal. Even the use of contrasted woods was frowned on, and the various exotic timbers so favoured during the Regency – such as zebra-wood, satinwood and amboyna – were discarded in favour of plain mahogany, rosewood or walnut, and oak for furniture in the gothic or Elizabethan taste. It should perhaps be emphasized that this preference for solid unadorned wood did not necessarily involve an increase in weight, for it is often possible to reduce both the size and weight by using solid timber in place of veneered surfaces on a separate core.

When we contrast this use of plain undecorated wood with the metal inlays and zoomorphic carving of the Regency, or with the inset porcelain medallions and embossed leather panels, which were so popular in the 1860's, we can see how wide of the mark is the belief that typical Early Victorian furniture must be over-ornamented and fussy. It may therefore be as well to confirm the point by a quotation from the most perceptive contemporary comment on Early Victorian furniture in general, namely Matthew Digby Wyatt's already mentioned *Report on the Furniture at the Paris Exhibition of 1855*. In his report he laments the conservative habits of the English cabinet-makers, who, for over a generation, had been content with "good joinery, glueing up, and mitering, smooth, plain, veneering, and clean but not intricate turning", and criticizes them severely for having deliberately turned their backs on more elaborate surface treatments with carving or marquetry.

The use of wood substitutes. Reference should perhaps be made here to the use of wood-substitutes. Perusal of the catalogue of the Great Exhibition, and even more of the catalogues of the four Society of Arts Exhibitions which preceded it, might lead to the conclusion that a great deal of Early Victorian furniture made use of patent materials such as gutta-percha, stamped leather, carton-pierre, Albano's canabic composition, and so on. The evidence of the Gillow records, however, supported by accounts of current trade methods such as the comprehensive report incorporated in Blackie's *Cabinet-Maker's Assistant*, 1853, show that, with the exception of papier-mâché, which is in rather a different category, these substitutes never had much currency. Perhaps the only decisive change in materials during this period arose from the universal introduction of Italian marble tops for washstands, and also to some extent for sideboards and chiffoniers, during the 1840's, as a result of price-reductions consequent on the perfection of steam-driven marble-cutting machines in the 1830's. The parallel efforts in the 1840's to popularize British substitutes such as the Derbyshire and Limerick near-marbles, and Magnus' patent painted slate, made no permanent impact, and ambitious projects like the fantastic slate-furniture at Penrhyn Castle must have been quite exceptional.

The use of machinery. A similar false impression results from assuming that the various wood-working machines, especially the patent carving machines of Irving, and of Taylor, Williams and Jordan, as demonstrated at these same exhibitions, were already in regular commercial use during this period and influenced in some way the design of Early Victorian furniture. There is very little evidence to support this view. It is true that Henry Cole, in the guise of *Felix Summerly's Art Manufactures*, attempted, as one would expect, to exploit Jordan's patent, with a fantastic arm-chair called "The Repose", which incorporated numerous figures designed by J. C. Horsley, the painter. It is also known that C. J. Richardson, the Elizabethan enthusiast, made designs especially for it. Neither the Gillow records nor the Blackie account, however, include any evidence of these mechanical developments. Moreover, the most authoritative contemporary report on the whole subject (a paper by G. L. Molesworth *On the Conversion of Wood by Machinery* to the Institute of Civil Engineers, 17 November, 1857) implies that regularly used machinery at

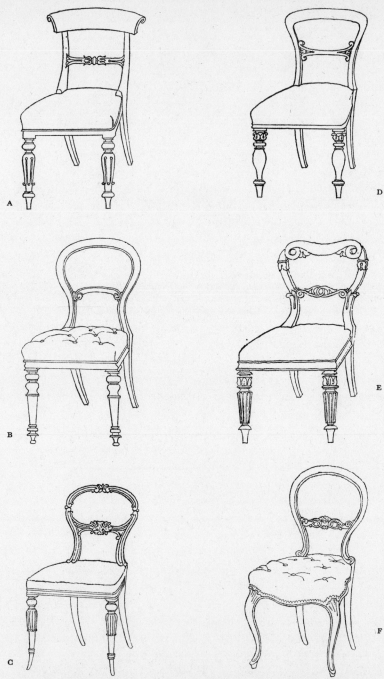

Fig. 42. The development of the balloon-back chair. (A), (B) and (C) are typical dining-room chairs, *c.* 1830, 1835 and 1850 respectively. (D), (E) and (F) are typical drawing-room chairs, *c.* 1830, 1835 and 1850 respectively.

that date was limited to circular- and band-saws, and planing and mortising machines, which could have had little influence on design. There is, however, some reason to believe that the increased use of fret-cutting in the 1850's may have been connected with the perfecting of Sandy and Powell's fret-cutting machinery.

Stylistic changes from 1850 to 60. These generalizations about the "Early Victorian style", are intended to apply to the whole period from 1835 to 1860. It must be admitted, however, that they require some slight qualifications when applied to new furniture designs produced after 1850. The most marked change thereafter was a tendency away from the completely upholstered chairs and sofas of the 1840's. Shapes remained unchanged, but the wooden framework was now usually visible rather than completely concealed as hitherto, and the incorporation of a little openwork carving, and especially fret-cutting, as just mentioned, became acceptable. Half-padded arms took their place beside the earlier fully-padded sides for easy-chairs. Visible legs were substituted for the solid box-upholstery of ottomans. These changes were not pronounced enough to invalidate the continued vitality of the Early Victorian style down to, and even beyond, 1860, but they anticipated further changes which began to gather momentum in the very last years of our period, and which ultimately affected a radical transformation of English furniture styles in the late 1860's.

All that can be said here is that the basis of this later transformation was a reversal to straight lines in reaction against the Early Victorian curve, and a revival of interest in every type of polychromatic surface-treatment after the long reign of undecorated French polish. Only one facet of this complex transformation was already becoming visible before 1860, namely the revival of Louis XVI styles. This revival was inaugurated at the Paris Exhibition of 1855, and was marked for English cabinet-makers in particular by a remarkable cabinet exhibited by Jackson and Graham, which gained them a "Medal of Honour". This splendid piece – it has unfortunately not proved possible to discover its present whereabouts – broke right away from early Victorian tradition. In the employment of French designers and modellers, in the use of satinwood and tulipwood in place of mahogany and rosewood, in the revival of marquetry and ormolu, and the incorporation of porcelain plaques, it fully anticipated all the characteristics of that elegant, elaborate style – sometimes thought of as a Sheraton revival – usually associated with the work of firms such as Wright and Mansfield or Holland and Sons in the 1860's and 1870's. Indeed, although one or two pattern-books published between 1855 and 1860 already incorporate a few "Louis XVI designs", and although percipient contemporary commentators such as Richard Redgrave (who curiously called it the "Gauthier" – though he presumably meant "Gouthière" – style) noticed the change; its general impact was hardly yet discernible, and the fully-fledged revival of this style can be legitimately placed beyond the limits of the Early Victorian period.

These conclusions about the Early Victorian style in general must now be applied in turn to the main categories of furniture.

Chairs. The Early Victorian period was responsible for two significant contributions to chair design. The first, and most important, was the development of the balloon-back chair. In 1830 this was entirely unknown; by 1860 it had become by far the commonest type both for dining- and drawing-rooms. The stages by which it developed during the intervening years can be traced fairly accurately, but it is very difficult to offer any satisfactory explanation as to why it appeared just when it did. Strangely enough, contemporary writers on furniture seem to have been completely unaware of this basic change, and it has not proved possible to trace even a single contemporary reference to it. All that can be said with confidence is that it was an indigenous English development, not taken over from France.

In 1830 almost all chairs were still of a uniform sub-classical pattern, with a broad horizontal yoke-rail extending well beyond the plain uprights (which merely continued upwards the line of the back legs), a much narrower carved horizontal splat, a padded seat, and straight front legs. In the case of dining-room or parlour chairs, variations of this standard pattern were limited to the carving of the splat and to the slight enrichment of the ends of the yoke-rail with volutes and the like. In the case of drawing-room chairs the basic classical type was being increasingly challenged by the recently revived Louis XIV style, which at the least involved carving the yoke-rail and splat with baroque scrolls, and at the most replacing them by an elaborately carved back entirely made up of contrasting scrolls. In either case the front seat-rail and legs remained straight, and there was as yet no return to the cabriole leg.

The balloon-back seems to have developed from the simultaneous modification after 1830 of both the yoke-rail dining-room type and the scroll-back drawing-room type. By 1835 we find dining-room versions in which the yoke-rail has been rounded-off and made continuous with the uprights, and at the same time a simplified drawing-room chair in which the scroll-carving has been almost eliminated, leaving a plain curved top. The step from these two types to the fully-fledged balloon-back was easily made in the next ten years.

Once established, the balloon-back rapidly became predominant, until by 1850 almost all trace of the classical yoke-rail had disappeared. It remained the standard pattern until the late 1860's, in a more austere form for the dining-room or library, and with carved enrichments within the basic rounded top for the drawing-room or boudoir. After 1850 cabriole legs usually replaced the earlier straight legs for the drawing-room versions.

Throughout this period bedroom or "fancy" chairs followed the same changes, but with a lighter build – mahogany being replaced by japanned or stained birch or maple, the padded seat being replaced by cane, and the flimsier legs being strengthened by double side-stretchers.

The second original contribution to chair-design was the tall-backed, short-legged, low-seated, entirely upholstered chair, sometimes called a "devotional", "prie-dieu" or "vesper" chair (Pl. 56). This typical example of attention to the functional requirements of comfort at the expense of appearance seems to have been derived from the cane-backed Charles II chair, which, owing to a curious and incomprehensible confusion, was thought by the early Elizabethan enthusiasts to be a typical sixteenth-century design. By 1840 it had developed in two different directions. On the one hand, the more ambitious designers, such as Bridgens and Whitaker, elaborated a whole series of tall-backed chairs with turned legs and uprights, and incorporating heavy strapwork carving – a type which was carried into the 1850's by Blackie's already-quoted *Cabinet-Makers' Assistant*. On the other hand, the humbler men such as Henry Wood transformed it into the typical Early Victorian drawing-room chair, covered in Berlin wool-work, and decorated with tassels and fringes. The earliest of these date from about 1835 and they remained in favour until after 1860 (Pl. 57). The specifically "devotional" version, as found for example in Henry Lawford's design books (1855), had a T-shaped tall back with a padded top-rest for use during family prayers.

The only other specifically Early Victorian chair style was the child's chair with straight tall back, tall legs and double-stretchers, called after Sir Astley Cooper (1768–1841), the anatomist on whose principles it was designed.

Sofas, couches, ottomans and easy-chairs. The Early Victorian emphasis on comfort rather than "style" can be traced very clearly in the design of sofas, couches and ottomans. In 1830 the standard sofa had a rectangular plan, with straight back, front-rail and ends, all at right-angles to each other. Moreover, although the back might be slightly canted and the ends might curve over, all the horizontal lines were also straight. The only relief to the austere impression was provided by slight carved or inlaid enrichments – usually in the form of the anthemion – to the front-rail and the front surface of the arms, and by the two cylindrical bolster-cushions.

For more opulent interiors this standard neo-classical form had, from 1827 onwards, to meet the competition of the more heavily ornamented revived Louis XIV sofa, which usually took the form of a basically classical shape with the addition of carved and gilt cresting. For more normal domestic use the neo-classic remained in favour until the late 1830's, and was then superseded not by the baroque or rococo scrolls of the French eighteenth century, but by a styleless Early Victorian compromise. This had a straight front rail and plain legs, but a back which was rounded in both elevation and plan and was structurally continuous with the ends or arms. The typical version of the 1840's, as seen in the Smee pattern-books for example, was padded all over, with no wood visible except in the diminutive legs, and variations in design were therefore limited to the outline of the back, which was sometimes humped up in the centre and sometimes at each end.

In the 1850's the basic shape remained unchanged, but there was now a tendency to reintroduce a visible wooden framework to the back and arms, and the single-, twin- or even triple-humped back often incorporated elaborately carved or fretworked open panels. The variant known as the "sociable", "conversation sofa", or "tête-à-tête", with the two ends facing each other on the lines of the French "causeuse" (Pl. 55B), was popular for a short time during the 1840's, but seems to have already gone out of favour by the mid-1850's. It provided the hack designers with opportunities for some of their most fanciful inventions.

Single-ended couches followed the same changes as sofas, with an emphasis during the 1830's on an entirely plain type with a slightly canted end, designed to support the back while reading. This seems first to have been evolved by Thomas King, but it was immediately taken over by the trade generally as an "Adelaide" couch.

Ottomans provided a more informal companion to the sofa throughout this period. Up to about 1845 the normal form was extremely simple, consisting merely of a plain free-standing upholstered box with a back and cushions, and with seats either on two or all four sides. By 1850 it had generally become more elaborate, with a visible wooden framework round the upholstery and with short legs in place of the previous box-base. A common pattern had the seat divided into compartments by arms, and sometimes the compartments formed individual segments which could be placed together or separately, as convenient. In the more pretentious examples the central back was surmounted by a *jardinière*.

Easy, or "lounging" chairs, as they were usually called, tended to follow the same lines of development as sofas, and may therefore conveniently be considered with them. The basic transformation from the rectangular version of the 1830's to the tubby and rounded style of the 1850's can more readily be illustrated than described. For a short time in the early 1850's there was a vogue for a particularly clumsy-looking type in which the back, although separated from the arms, was joined to them by a separate member running from the cresting down to the arm-rest. The only other type deserving mention was the library-chair with the normal back and arms replaced by a heavily padded continuous horizontal semi-circle. This first appears in the 1840's with the semi-circle supported only in the centre, but by 1860 it had been modified so that the padded semi-circle was supported by turned balusters round its whole length, and as such remained a standard type until well into the twentieth century.

Tables. By comparison with other articles of furniture, tables afford little evidence of changes in Early Victorian taste. The standard extending dining-room table, the various types of occasional table, the ingenious rising side-tables operated with pulley and weights on the principle of the sash-window, and even the drawing-room work-table with pouch, altered comparatively little during the thirty years under review. Only the circular loo-table showed significant changes, which took

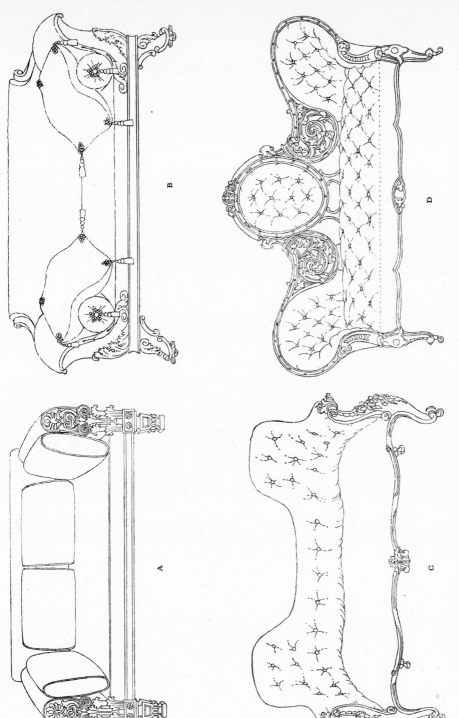

Fig. 43. The development of the Early Victorian sofa. (A) Grecian style, *c.* 1830, (B) Louis XIV style, *c.* 1835, (C) and (D) two typical Victorian styles, *c.* 1845 and 1860 respectively.

two forms. In the first place, there was a tendency in the 1850's to enrich the top, which from 1830 to 1850 had normally been completely plain, either with a gadrooned moulding or with a scalloped outline. In the second place, the standard 1830 type with a clearly differentiated supporting pedestal – usually pyramidical– resting on a flat triangular block, itself often standing on claw or paw feet, slowly evolved over the next twenty years, until by 1850 it was normal for the three legs to flow directly from the central column in loose and relaxed curves which typify the more spineless qualities of the Early Victorian style. In the 1850's a more elaborate support, with a central column supplemented by three or four thinner ones, was introduced, and is found not only in the designs of men like Peter Thomson and John Dwyer, but even in the cheaper pattern-books. There seems little doubt that this is a case where a design originally evolved as suitable for cast iron, was later taken over and translated into wood.

In considering all Early Victorian tables, it must never be forgotten that, as A. J. Downing put it in 1850, "they depend for this good effect mainly on the drapery or cover of handsome cloth or stuff usually spread upon their top and concealing all but the lower part of the legs" (*The Architecture of Country Houses*).

Sideboards and chiffoniers. The development of the sideboard during this period gives us the clearest evidence of that tendency to round off all angularities which we have claimed as one of the most typical manifestations of the Early Victorian style. Throughout the whole period the pedestal type of sideboard was the standard pattern for normal domestic purposes, with open-legged types rarely used. In 1830 the shape was rigidly rectangular, with a low wooden rectangular backboard. By 1840 backs were being made higher and were beginning to incorporate mirrors, which usually followed the threefold division of the base, with a larger mirror in the centre, flanked by two smaller ones over the pedestals – still with rectangular outlines. By 1850 backs were higher still, and it became customary to raise the centre mirror above the flanking ones and to give all three semi-circular rather than rectangular crestings. By 1860 it was more common for the whole back to be merged into a single semi-circular mirror. Precisely the same development affected the pedestals, though with a time-lag, and it was not until after 1850 that the change towards a semi-circular elevation for the sideboard was paralleled by a semi-circular plan also, with the outer angles of the pedestals rounded off.

The same changes can be traced even more clearly in the more modest chiffonier which was regarded as the appropriate article for a dining-room which was too small or unpretentious for a full-scale sideboard. As an anonymous domestic manual of 1851 (*How to Furnish a House and Make it a Home*), points out, a sideboard with pedestals looks ridiculous if less than about 4 ft. wide, whereas a chiffonier, with its solid front, could reasonably be as small as 3 ft. wide. The standard type in the 1830's had a small shelf projecting from the wooden backboard, and supported on turned balusters or Louis XIV trusses, according to taste. There were usually two cupboards in front, with wire-grille doors backed with pleated silk. More elaborate examples incorporated a set of small bookshelves. As with the sideboards, the wooden backboard was gradually replaced by a mirror-back, the pleated silk was replaced by wooden or glass doors, the plan became semi-circular, and curved open shelves were fitted on either side of the central cupboards.

When we turn to the more pretentious designs, either for sideboards or chiffoniers, we find a particularly rich crop of "Elizabethan" examples. Whereas the first enthusiasm for the revived Louis XIV and XV styles during the years 1827–35 found its most natural expression in upholstered drawing-room furniture, the Elizabethan, with its emphasis on heavily carved solid oak, was thought to be especially well adapted to the more manly articles such as sideboards or buffets. The first examples, in the early 1830's, were merely reproductions of original Jacobean pieces. By 1838, however, we find men like Bridgens designing original Elizabethan sideboards covered with carved strapwork for their rich clients (such as James Watt, the then owner of Aston Hall), and even the conservative firm of Gillow produced in 1841 a whole suite of most elaborately carved furniture in the Elizabethan style for the Richmond-Gale-Braddyll family of Conishead Priory. Every pattern-book of the 1840's, such as those of Henry Wood, automatically contained some elaborately carved Elizabethan sideboards, and these were continued into the 1850's also by Peter Thomson and others. The only slight change after 1850 – no doubt stimulated by the Great Exhibition – was for plain strapwork to be enlivened by the incorporation of naturalistic carved ornament usually with a "literary-functionalist" flavour. In the case of sideboards this required the introduction of dead game, fishing-tackle, grapes and the like, as the appropriate symbols. Apart from the few first-class examples, which have already been referred to in connection with the Warwick school, this trend produced little of merit, for the carving is almost always perfunctory and mechanical.

Miscellaneous furniture. Of the many miscellaneous articles of furniture which made up the typical Victorian home, not much need be said. Certain types which were in regular use up to the 1830's, then virtually disappeared – such as the semi-circular wine-table, the ubiquitous Regency tripod-stand, the commode and (after about 1840) the classical hall-couch. Other types, such as footstools, firescreens (Pls. 60A, 62B), work-tables and flower-stands, continued in use and faithfully reflected the changes of taste already mentioned for the more important items. Still others, such as davenports, table-flap cases, Canterburies, music-stools and portfolio-stands, changed little throughout the period.

Almost the only article of furniture which first sprang into regular use during this period was the what-not. Although known earlier, it only became a standard article after about 1840. The only change worth mentioning is that after about 1855 the earlier free-standing type takes second place to the later corner variety.

Gothic furniture. Gothic furniture requires separate mention, for throughout this period it remained rather isolated from normal furniture fashions. It was rarely regarded as appropriate for rooms other than the hall or library, or exceptionally for panelled rooms in old houses. The production of a whole range of gothic furniture, such as that designed for Snelston Hall, Derbyshire, by L. N. Cottingham, the antiquarian, in 1844 (Pl. 55A), was quite exceptional. Normally speaking, the term merely implied a superficial tracery-pattern on the back of a hall-seat, or the incorporation of linen-fold panelling into a library settle. For obvious reasons the Elizabethan revival in the 1830's led to a good deal of confusion with the gothic, and in many pattern-books of the 1840's it would be quite impossible, were it not for the captions, to know which style was intended.

It does not seem that the publication of A. W. N. Pugin's *Gothic Furniture* in 1835, and his many other efforts to propagate a true understanding of Gothic principles, had any marked effect on general furniture production; presumably because his admonitions appeared to be addressed mainly to architects and because the excellent and chaste gothic furniture (Pl. 52B) which he himself designed for several of his clients was never illustrated. The only sign of his influence was the elaborate gothic furniture which J. G. Crace – who had previously worked in entirely different styles – began to produce at the end of the 1840's, and which is typified by the well-known bookcase, supposedly to Pugin's own design, exhibited in the Medieval Court of the 1851 Exhibition, and now in the Victoria and Albert Museum, a remarkable range of pieces which he produced for Sir James Watts of Abney Hall near Stockport, in 1847, and an imposing piece which earned him an award at the Paris Exhibition of 1855.

Metal furniture. Metal furniture also requires separate mention. It falls into two categories. The first comprises cast-iron garden-furniture and hall furniture such as hat and umbrella stands and flower stands. This was made as a by-product of their normal industrial work by iron foundries such as Coalbrookdale, Shropshire, the Carron Company, Stirlingshire, and various smaller foundries in the area around Birmingham, such as Archibald Kendrick of Walsall, and Thomas Marsh of Dudley. It was already in production before 1830, but had a particular vogue between 1845 and 1855. During this period Coalbrookdale especially made great efforts to produce a full range of indoor cast-iron furniture, including pieces for living-rooms upholstered in damask or velvet. The majority were designed by Charles Crooke, but they also called in outside artists. Judging from contemporary illustrations of examples such as the "hall stand for hats, cloaks, umbrellas, with looking glass, lamp, letter and brush box, and inkstand all combined", designed "after a suggestion by Felix Summerly", which won a Gold Isis medal from the Society of Arts in 1849, and the "deer-hound table" designed by John Bell, the popular sculptor, for the Paris Exhibition of 1855, one may hope that these ludicrous and impractical examples have all long since disappeared. The present-day habit of painting surviving pieces white may help to conceal their inherent ugliness, but at the cost of falsifying their original appearance, for they were normally produced in only three finishes: "Berlin-black, bronzed, or japanned in imitation of oak".

The second category consisted of brass furniture, produced by a different section of the Birmingham trade, namely the brass-foundries, who added beds to their traditional output of cornice-poles, fenders and the like. Although brass beds were being manufactured by 1825, they made so little impact at first that as late as 1844 the "Art Union" reported the French metal furniture shown at the Paris Exhibition of that year as a great novelty. After about 1845, however, there was a spurt in Birmingham production, mainly as a result of Peyton and Harlow's patent (1841) for taper tubing. Their main competitor was R. W. Winfield, who produced some very attractive ornamental brass beds in the late 1840's.

In addition to these two main categories, there was also during this period a certain amount of experimental metal furniture, ranging from Mallet's preposterous chairs made of riveted gas-tubing, sponsored by J. C. Loudon in the 1830's, to elegant and practical pieces in square-section or strip brass.

Papier-mâché furniture. Although it is papier-mâché furniture which most readily comes to mind when the Early Victorian period is in question, it would be quite wrong to suppose that it was as frequently found in the average Early Victorian home as it now is in second-hand shops or in "period rooms" in museums. The fact that the bulk of papier-mâché furniture can safely be assumed to be Early Victorian, that marked pieces are fairly common, and that its pictorial decoration makes it susceptible to classification into various sub-groupings, has contributed to invest it with an exaggerated importance. If allowance is made for the fact that almost all the more attractive examples were made by the single firm of Jennens and Bettridge, and that both they and the other leading firms such as Loveridge, Thomas Farmer, Dean and Benson, and Footherape, Showell and Shenton of Birmingham, and Walton of Wolverhampton, were mainly occupied in making trays and boxes rather than movable furniture as such, it is statistically obvious that the total output of papier-mâché furniture must always have formed a very small fraction of the wood furniture turned out by cabinet-makers in every large town in the country. It is, indeed, symptomatic that none of the half-dozen or so domestic and house-keeping manuals in general circulation before 1860 mention papier-mâché furniture at all.

There is only space here to mention the two main technical developments which influenced the appearance of the furniture. Both are to the credit of Jennens and Bettridge. In 1825 they patented the use of pearl-shell in papier-mâché decoration, and in 1847 of so-called "gem-inlaying". Both processes are found applied not only to papier-mâché proper, but also to the stained and painted wooden furniture which is often confused with it.

For Further Reading

Cabinet Dictionary, by Thomas Sheraton, 1803.

The Dictionary of English Furniture, by P. MacQuoid and Ralph Edwards (3 vols., 1924–7); revised by Ralph Edwards, Country Life, London, 1954.

English Decoration and Furniture of the Early Renaissance (1500–1650), by Margaret Jourdain, Batsford, 1924.

Furniture-Making in Seventeenth and Eighteenth Century England, by R. W. Symonds, Connoisseur, London, 1955.

Furniture in England from 1660 to 1760, by Francis Lenygon, 1914; revised by Margaret Jourdain, Batsford, 1925.

The Gentleman and Cabinet-Maker's Director, by Thomas Chippendale, Connoisseur, London, and Taplinger, New York, 1957.

Georgian Cabinet-Makers, by Ralph Edwards and Margaret Jourdain, revised edition, Country Life, London, and O.U.P., New York, 1955.

The Gothic Revival, by Sir Kenneth Clark, Constable, London, 1950.

Regency Antiques, by Brian Reade, Batsford, London, 1953.

Regency Furniture, by Margaret Jourdain, revised edition, Country Life, London, 1949.

A Treatise of Japaning and Varnishing, by J. Stalker and G. Parker, 1688.

The Work of William Kent, by Margaret Jourdain, Country Life, London, 1948.

The Concise Encyclopædia of Antiques, Vols. 1–5, Connoisseur, London, and Hawthorn, New York, 1955–61.

Index

PLATE 1A. A hutch table of oak with doors carved with a tracery design, the centre panel carved with a floreated pattern. *Private Collection.*

PLATE 1B. Carved oak joyned stool, of the late sixteenth century. *S. W. Wolsey.*

PLATE 2. Carved oak armchair inlaid with holly and bog oak, dated 1596.
S. W. Wolsey.

PLATE 3A. An early example of a sixteenth-century table with three trestle supports and stretcher rail.

PLATE 3B. An Elizabethan table with drawing leaves and carved bulbous supports.
Hart Collection.

PLATE 4A. A five-sided cup-board with an aumbry, of the early sixteenth century. *Sir William Burrell Collection.*

PLATE 4B. English oak counter or rent table, early sixteenth century. *Peter Gwynn Collection.*

PLATE 5. Oak open court cup-board with two frieze drawers and carved heraldic animal and figure supports, late sixteenth century. *Sir William Burrell Collection.*

Plate 6a. Small panelled oak cup-board with two doors. Late sixteenth century. *Peter Gwynn Collection.*

Plate 6b. A rare type of late sixteenth-century court or plate cup-board. *Hart Collection.*

PLATE 7A. Oak press cup-board
ornamented with turning, carv·
ing and inlay, *c.* 1600.
Hart Collection.

PLATE 7B. Small late six-
teenth-century games table,
with two folding extensions to
the top. *Hart Collection.*

PLATE 8. Headboard of an oak carved and painted late sixteenth-century four-post bed; the acanthus-decorated frieze brackets in walnut. *L. G. G. Ramsey Collection.*

PLATE 9B. Oak press cupboard. The recessed upper part has two cupboards, separated by pilasters framing a central panel with carved arch, the lower part a cupboard with shelf, enclosed by panelled doors. 1610. *Victoria and Albert Museum.*

PLATE 9A. Oak press cupboard, with drawers below, and panelled sides. Late seventeenth or early eighteenth century. *Private Collection.*

PLATE 10A. "Folding" table of oak, with one movable gate. *c.* 1650. *Hart Collection.*

PLATE 10B. Hanging livery or food cupboard, enclosed doors each with a row of turned balusters above a panel de ated with lozenges; the frieze carved with guilloche ornan Mid-seventeenth century. *Private Collection.*

PLATE 10C. Draw table, the legs of bulbous form, tied by plain stretchers. Length (unextended) 6 ft. 9 in. Se half of seventeenth century. *The Oak House Museum, West Bromwich, Staffs.*

PLATE IIA. "Farthingale" chair of walnut, the front
gs of columnar form. Height 3 ft.; width 1 ft. 10 in.
irst quarter of seventeenth century. *Victoria and
lbert Museum.* IIB. (*right*) Carved and turned oak
chair, Lancashire type. Dated 1641.
Victoria and Albert Museum.

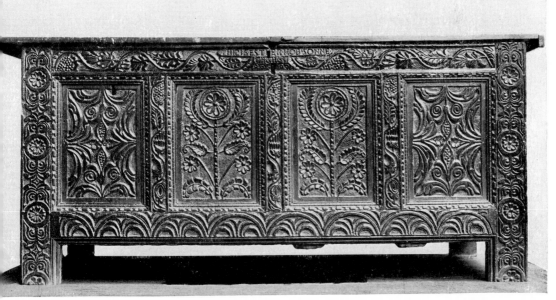

LATE IIC. Chest, panelled and elaborately carved with conventional ornament. Height 2 ft. 5½ in.; width 5 ft. 6 in.
From Lincolnshire, dated 1637. *Victoria and Albert Museum.*

PLATE 12A. Settle-table, the lower part in the form of a chest. The table top is attached to the backs of the arms by wooden pegs, and serves, when raised, as a back to the settle. Length 5 ft. 11 in. Mid-seventeenth century. *Victoria and Albert Museum.*

PLATE 12B. Oak armchair, the back inlaid with an arabesque design within an arch and surmounted by a scrolled cresting; the framing uprights decorated with applied split balusters, flanked by scrolled "ear-pieces". Mid-seventeenth century.
Victoria and Albert Museum.

PLATE 12C. Oak chest of drawers, on a low stand with twist-turned supports tied by stretchers; the drawer fronts decorated with panels of raised mouldings. Height 4 ft. 4½ in. Late seventeenth century.
Victoria and Albert Museum.

PLATE 13. Carved and gilt table with decoration of gilt
gesso. Height 2 ft. 6½ in.; length 3 ft. 6 in. About 1700.
Victoria and Albert Museum.

PLATE 14. Walnut side-table, decorated with arabesque
marquetry and fitted with one long drawer in the frieze;
twist-turned legs tied by flat curved stretchers with an
oval marquetry panel in the centre. Last quarter of the
seventeenth century.

PLATE 15. Walnut gate-leg table, the oval top supported on turned legs with shaped feet. Height 2 ft. 4 in. Late seventeenth century. *Victoria and Albert Museum.*

PLATE 16B. Burr mulberry bureau bookcase, with inlaid pewter stringing lines. Attributed to Coxed and Woster.

PLATE 16A. State bed, upholstered in red and gold brocade. From Wroxton Abbey, Oxfordshire. Late seventeenth century.

PLATE 17B. Dressing glass, japanned red and gold. The sloping front of the base is hinged and opens to disclose an arrangement of small drawers and pigeon holes, cupboard in centre. Height 3 ft. 3 in. Early eighteenth century.

PLATE 17A. Mirror frame, overlaid with incised oriental lacquer, c. 1675. *Victoria and Albert Museum.*

PLATE 18A. Walnut winged arm-chair, upholstered and covered with silk needlework; the cabriole front legs, carved on the knee with a shell, are hipped and finished in modified hoof feet. Early eighteenth century. *Formerly in the Hart Collection. Now at Colonial Williamsburg.*

PLATE 18B. Upholstered chair with walnut framework; the high back surmounted by a foliated cresting carved in openwork; the turned legs are joined by shaped cross stretchers with a finial. End of the seventeenth century. *Victoria and Albert Museum.*

PLATE 18C. Cane settee of double chair design, supported in front by scrolled legs joined by deep scrolled rails; the uprights to the back and the stretchers are of turned baluster form, *c.* 1700. *Hart Collection.*

PLATE 19. The Stone Hall, Houghton, Norfolk, showing furniture designed by William Kent, *c.* 1725.

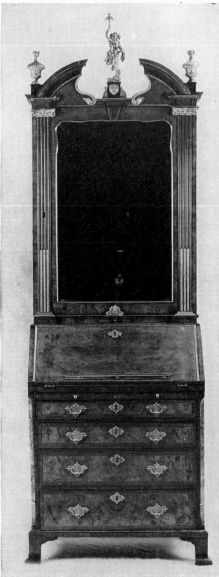

PLATE 20A. Mirror in gilt gesso
frame, with shell ornament on the
cresting, *c.* 1715. *Hart Collection.*

PLATE 20B. Walnut bureau-cabinet,
c. 1725. *R. H. Heathcoat Amory, Esq.*

PLATE 21. Mirror in a carved and gilt frame in the rococo taste, *c.* 1755, reflecting an overmantel mirror in a frame designed by William Kent, *c.* 1725. *Courtesy the Marquess of Cholmondeley.*

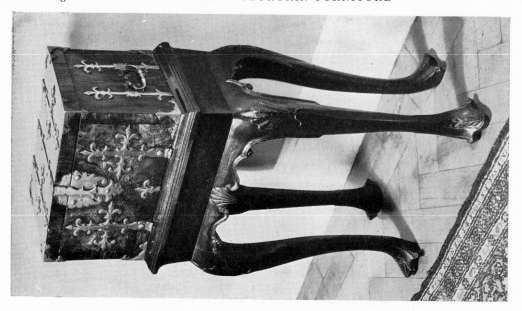

PLATE 22B. Late seventeenth-century walnut brass-bound casket (Flemish) on a George II period carved

PLATE 22A. Mahogany tea-table with scalloped top and tripod base, c. 1745.
Hart Collection.

PLATE 23. The Supper Room, Governor's Palace, Williamsburg, Virginia, with English furniture, c. 1710–60, taken to America by Colonial Governors.

PLATES 24A & B. One of a [pair]
of pier tables (*c.* 1710–20)
silvered gesso work, the [top]
decorated (*see below*) with [the]
entwined cypher – H.W. [and]
W.H. – of the original ow[ners.]
These tables are highly exc[ep]-
tional because they are silve[red]
and not gilded, there being v[ery]
little silvered gesso furni[ture]
extant. The silvering of g[esso]
work instead of gilding [was]
practised by the carvers [and]
gilders of the time of Qu[een]
Anne and George I in orde[r to]
give furniture the appeara[nce]
of being made of real sil[ver.]
James Moore (16?–1726), w[ho,]
in partnership with John G[um]-
ley, was one of the R[oyal]
cabinet-makers to the Cr[own]
in the reign of George [I,]
appears to have specialize[d in]
the making of gesso furnit[ure.]
At Hampton Court and B[uck]-
ingham Palaces there are s[ome]
gesso stands and tables of [high]
quality which bear his sig[na]-
ture on the top. *Hart Colle[ction]*

PLATE 25A. Mahogany serpentine-fronted commode, with rococo influence in the carving and handles, *c.* 1750. *Christie's.*

PLATE 25B. Mahogany side table with marble top, *c.* 1745. *Victoria and Albert Museum.*

PLATE 26A. Mahogany chair with latticework back in the Chinese taste, *c.* 1760.

PLATE 26B. Windsor chair with turned bars in back, *c.* 1750.

PLATE 26C. Mahogany armchair, *c.* 1755. *Frank Partridge, Inc., New York.*

PLATE 26D. Upholstered walnut armchair with fou finely carved cabriole legs, *c.* 1745. *Needham's Antiques New York.*

PLATE 27. Mahogany bookcase, attributed to Thomas Chippendale, *c.* 1760. *The Lord Herbert.*

PLATE 28A. Japanned black and gold dressing commode, probably by Chippendale,
c. 1750. *Victoria and Albert Museum.*

PLATE 28B. Walnut card table with folding top, c. 1750. *Hart Collection.*

PLATE 29A. Mahogany cabinet
and writing table, with carved
rococo ornament, *c.* 1760.
Messrs Ackermann.

PLATE 29B. Mahogany pedestal library table, *c.* 1750.

PLATE 30. Mahogany bureau bookcase with carving in the rococo taste, attributed to Thomas Chippendale, *c.* 1760. *The Lord Herbert.*

PLATE 31A. An example of portable furniture: a travelling chair bed made by Thomas Butler, *c.* 1790, and carrying his label.

PLATE 31B. A sculptor's mahogany adjustable modelling table, *c.* 1775.

PLATE 31C. Mahogany library wheelbarrow with shaped sides and curved arms, early nineteenth century.
Lord Fairhaven Collection.

PLATE 32A. Mahogany shield-back armchair, decorated with paterae and foliage in holly wood, *c.* 1870. *Earl of Yarborough Collection.*

PLATE 32B. Mahogany armchair, with splat work of carved drapery, *c.* 1785.

PLATE 32C. Rosewood armchair, with turned front legs, stretchers, arm supports and cresting rail. Note the panel of cane in the back, *c.* 1800.

PLATE 32D. Armchair with painted floral designs, turn legs and arm supports, and cane seat. *c.* 1795. *Col. J.* *Wadmore Collection.*

PLATE 33A. Commode, veneered and inlaid with various woods, *c.* 1765.
Formerly Earl of Shaftesbury Collection.

PLATE 33B. Regency bookcase inlaid with brass. Its low height is due to the fashion of leaving the walls free for pictures. *Metropolitan Museum, New York.*

PLATE 34A. Bow-fronted mahogany sideboard, with
satinwood inlay, late eighteenth century.

PLATE 34B. Pembroke table with
cross-banded top and reeded legs.

PLATE 34C. Pedestal and urn, with carved
and inlaid neo-classic decoration. Part of a
dining-room suite, *c.* 1775.

PLATE 35A. Regency rosewood sofa table with curved and reeded legs, brass feet and turned stretcher.

PLATE 35B. Carved and inlaid mahogany side-table, part of a dining-room suite, *c.* 1775.

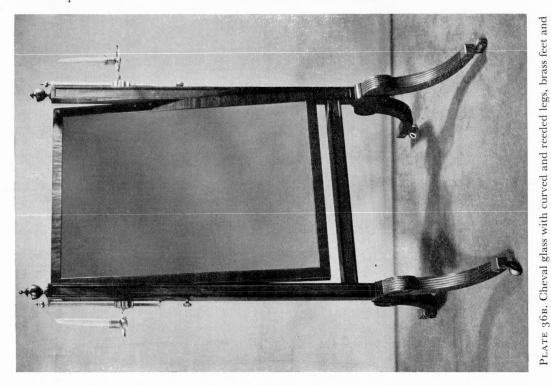

PLATE 36B. Cheval glass with curved and reeded legs, brass feet and brass sconces, c. 1800.

PLATE 36A. Pier glass surmounted by a classical urn and leaf motif. Below, a commode, inlaid in neo-classic taste. *West*

PLATE 37. The Drawing Room, West Wycombe Park, Buckinghamshire, showing upholstered chairs in the French style, popular in the Adam period. *West Wycombe Park, National Trust.*

PLATE 38A. Regency circular table inlaid with brass, showing the prevailing pillar-and-claw support.

PLATE 38B. Painted tripod table with hinged top and curved feet, *c*. 1795. *Col. J. M. Wadmore Collection.*

PLATE 38C. Cabinet, *c*. 1770. Attributed to Chippendale and Haig. *Viscount and Viscountess Gage Collection at Firle Place.*

PLATE 39A. Chair japanned in black and gold in the Chinese taste, *c.* 1810.

PLATE 39B. Mahogany chair with lyre-shaped splat, *c.* 1800.

PLATE 39C. Mahogany armchair with spiral reeding on the rails in back, *c.* 1810.

PLATE 39D. Japanned chair with panel painted in the Chinese taste, *c.* 1810.

PLATE 40A. Mahogany sofa table inlaid with brass; pedestal supported by a platform on splayed feet, *c.* 1815.
J. W. Evill Collection.

PLATE 40B. Mahogany pedestal library table, with ebonized stringing on the drawer fronts, *c.* 1815.

PLATE 41A. Mahogany extending dining table, on a central pillar-and-claw: two of the reeded end legs swing out to give space for extra leaves, *c.* 1820.

PLATE 41B. Rosewood architect's table, inlaid with brass. The miniature table folds up and shuts away as a drawer, *c.* 1810.

PLATE 42A. Mahogany circular pillar-and-claw dining table, showing method of adding leaves,
c. 1815–20.

PLATE 42B. Mahogany side table inlaid with brass, supported by lion monopodia, in the Egyptian
taste, *c.* 1810.

PLATE 43A. Rosewood side table, with ormolu mounts, marble top, and supports in the Egyptian taste, c. 1810.

PLATE 43B. Mahogany side table with carved paw feet, ormolu mounts and brass gallery, c. 1810.

PLATE 44. The Chinese taste: two stands, painted ivory, with mounts of ormolu and carved wood, gilt, and white
marble tops. Made for the Saloon at the Royal Pavilion, Brighton, about 1822. (*On permanent loan to the Royal*

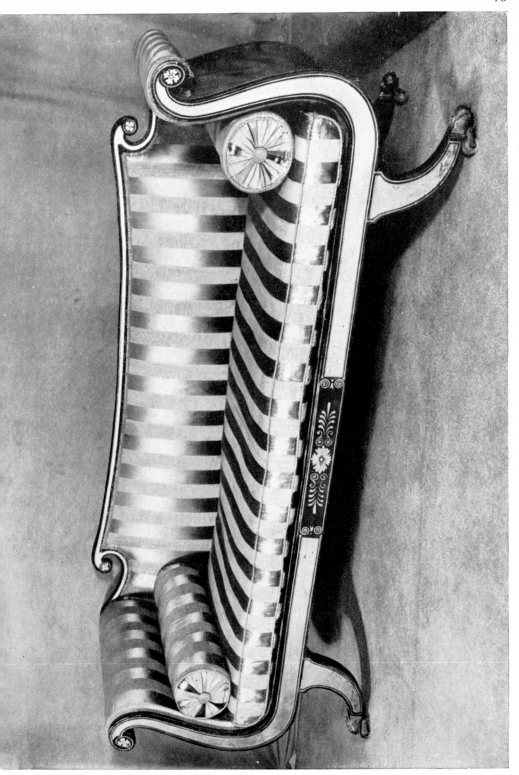

PLATE 45. Painted and gilt sofa, with brass paw feet on the outward-curving legs, c. 1810. *Victoria and Albert Museum.*

PLATE 46A. Rosewood cabinet with marble top, lion masks and feet and brass trellis doors and sides, c. 1810.

PLATE 46B. Mahogany music-stand ("Canterbury"), c. 1810.

PLATE 47A. Chiffonier "used chiefly for such books as are in constant use" (G. Smith, 1808). Lotus and anthemion decoration, paw feet and brass trellis door, c. 1810.

PLATE 47B. Small rosewood bookcase on stand, showing characteristic turning and brass decoration, c. 1810.

PLATE 48. English commode with marked French influence; boulle work panels, *c.* 1800–10.

PLATE 49. Mahogany side-table with imitation bamboo decoration in the Chinese taste, c. 1810.

PLATE 50. One of a set of four painted satinwood armchairs with panels of flowers and cupids and with cane seats, *c.* 1810. *In the collection of Mr and Mrs Frederick Poke.*

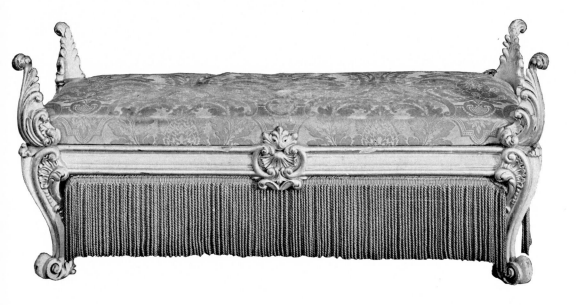

PLATES 51A & 51B. Carved and gilt couch and sofa in the Louis XIV style. Made by W. and C. Wilkinson, under the supervision of Philip Hardwick, for the Court Drawing-room, Goldsmiths' Hall, 1834.

PLATE 52A. Carved and padded chair, made by W. and C. Wilkinson, under the supervision of Philip Hardwick, for the Court Dining-room, Goldsmiths' Hall, 1834.

PLATE 52B. Carved and padded arm-chair, designed by A. W. N. Pugin for Scarisbrick Hall, 1835.

PLATE 53A. Side-table, made by W. and C. Wilkinson, under the supervision of Philip Hardwick, for the Court Room, Goldsmiths' Hall, 1834.

PLATE 53B. Sideboard designed by Henry Whitaker for the Conservative Club (now the Bath Club), 1844.

PLATE 54. Table with inlaid amboyna top, designed by Henry Whitaker for the Conservative Club (now the Bath Club), 1844.

PLATE 55A. Original design for carved and painted "gothic" sofa for Snelston Hall, Derbyshire, by Lewis Nockalls Cottingham, 1844.

PLATE 55B. Sofa ("Sociable") with double swivel ends, covered in silk damask woven by Baily
and Jackson of Spitalfields. *Stoneleigh Abbey, Warwickshire, c.* 1844.

PLATE 56. Turned "prie-dieu" chair, with tent-stitch embroidery on wool. *Charlecote Park, Warwickshire, c.* 1845.

PLATE 57. "Elizabethan" chair, with tent-stitch
embroidery on wool, *c.* 1845.

PLATE 58. Carved and gilt chair, made by W. and C.
Wilkinson, under the supervision of Philip Hardwick, for the
Court Drawing-room, Goldsmiths' Hall, 1834.

PLATE 59. Carved and inlaid chair, with inset porcelain plaque
depicting Queen Victoria. Designed and made by Henry Eyles
of Bath for the Great Exhibition, 1851.
Victoria and Albert Museum.

PLATE 60B. Carved and gilt chair, with back and seat of Berlin

PLATE 60A. "Elizabethan" fire-screen with panel of

PLATE 61. Sideboard, designed by Hugeus Protat and made by William Cookes of Warwick for Alscot Park, Warwickshire, 1853. *Courtesy Mrs Alston-Roberts-West.*

PLATE 62A. Carved and gilt music stool in the
"naturalistic style", with seat in Berlin wool-work.
Charlecote Park, Warwickshire, c. 1855.

PLATE 62B. Fire-screen designed and carved in the
"naturalistic style", by William Kendall of Warwick.
Stoneleigh Abbey, Warwickshire, 1858.

PLATE 63. Sideboard designed and carved in the "naturalistic style", by William Kendall of Warwick. *Stoneleigh Abbey, Warwickshire*, 1858.

PLATE 64. Sideboard, designed and carved by James Morris Willcox of Warwick. *Charlecote Park, Warwickshi* 1858.